BUILT to Fly

Stories to touch your heart, motivate your mind, and
inspire you to soar as God designed you to do

ERIC SCOFIELD

CONTENTS

This book is dedicated to my "of course" people.

(See Mark 1:41 in JB Phillips)

Marni, Hudson, Charlie, and Richard King Brown.

Love you, EJS

Remember—you are built to fly, and God designed you to soar!

PART I:
THE DIFFERENCE MAKER

....

*Difference makers can be people or they can be <u>attitudes</u>
that change our way of thinking. However they come to us,
they slap us upside the head and forever make us look at
life in a new way.*

THE GUY IN THE OTHER BUNK

Some people are like Sequoia trees. They make us look *up*. They make us look at life in a new and higher way. One year, I ran into one of those Sequoias during a meeting of our regional directors in Colorado Springs, Colorado.

That summer, we were staying not at a hotel but at the summer getaway of a Texan who had built the home just for his grandkids. He wanted to give them a fun place to spend their vacation with Grandpa and Grandma. Sweet!

As we hauled in our suitcases, we had to admit that this summer home was more interesting than any setup with a lobby and maid service. The house was built like a kid's playground, right on a golf course and overlooking the majestic Garden of the Gods Park in Colorado Springs. The incredible views were complimented by an outdoor fire pit for evening conversations and an indoor basketball court for friendly competition. To complete the playful vibe, the light switches were about three feet above the floor, as if the owner never expected his grandkids to grow up.

At the time, I was regional director in Houston, and because I was one of the younger guys, I ended up assigned to the kids' room with the bunkbeds. Probably because he was the nicest and most humble guy, John, another regional director, ended up with the bunkbeds, too.

1

Everybody else had their own private room. My new bunk buddy and I joked that it was like being banished to the kids' table on Thanksgiving, but we figured that as long as we had a place to sleep, we were glad to be coming to this divisional meeting.

So, there we were, two semi-strangers unpacking in a kids' bunk-room, stumbling over each other's shoes, fumbling for the light switches three feet off the floor, and joking about the bunkbeds ("Glad there's two of 'em. I wasn't looking forward to climbing a ladder tonight ..."). Finally, we were ready to turn in. I climbed into the bottom of my bunkbed on one side of the room, and John climbed into the bottom bunk on the other side of the room.

Then that awkward thing started—you know that weird, high school sleepover thing, where everybody tries to stay awake to show they've got their act together and are too cool to need sleep? This was kind of like that. Here we are, two grown guys lying in the dark on opposite sides of the room, both of us probably wondering how long we needed to chit-chat to sound polished and professional, and not like two geezers fighting to keep our eyes open.

Anyway, we chatted for a while, and finally, I said, "Hey, you ready to go to sleep?"

"Yeah, sounds good," John said, and with that, we turned out the lights.

And then, lying there in the dark, I started to think: "What is it with this guy? Why is he so different? His life looks so together ..."

From our simple chats throughout the day, I had picked up on stuff. John was from Kansas. His wife loved him; that was clear from the way he spoke about her. He was involved with his kid's life; I could tell that from the phone calls he made to his son. He didn't hide their conversations, so I could tell there was an easygoing affection between them.

I guessed he was about forty-five, while I was ten years younger. My son, Hudson, was still a toddler, and his son was turning thirteen. I was at that stage in life where you're still figuring out stuff, and I could see John had *direction* in his life. He had a direction as he parented. He had a direction as a husband. He had a direction in his job. It just felt like there was an anchor or a compass that was beyond what a normal person has. We had enough in common for sure, but he was that much ahead of me on the path that he could help point the way ahead. I could see my life twelve years ahead through his life.

So finally, right there, in the dark, I blurted out, "John, what is it about you? Why are you so different?"

I heard him chuckle on the other side of the room. "C'mon! Me? There's nothing different about me!"

"No, no, you obviously have a good marriage, and your kid likes being around you, which isn't so usual with a teenager. Just today, at the meeting, I've noticed that everybody has respect for you and your work. And there's a peace about you. What's your secret?"

My questions fell into the darkness and hung there so long that I thought maybe John was sick of talking. Then I heard him say, "Well, there *is* one thing, but I don't know if this is why I'm different. It started about fifteen years ago."

I don't know what I expected him to say next, but what he *did* say, sure wasn't it: "I have a covenant group."

A *what?* I had been involved with Young Life since I was a kid, and sure, I knew covenant in the biblical concept of God creating a covenant with man, an unbreakable bond that would last into eternity. But a covenant *group*? That was a new one.

"Well, it's a group of seven guys I meet with every year at the same time," John said. "We meet for three days. We've done the same thing every single year for fifteen years."

He was drawing me in. "Yeah? Tell me more."

The first year, John said, they set up the ground rules for the group. Here's what was so unusual about it: unlike most groups, their founding principles were not based on their interaction with *each other*—playing poker, smoking cigars, golfing, fishing, just the usual guy stuff—no, their group was about sharing the things in your life that need focus and attention, first and foremost your wife and kids, then, your co-workers and other people who are significant in your life, and of course, always being aware of what you need to work on, yourself. Most importantly, we talked about our spiritual goals and, for us, the value of walking with the Lord.

John explained, "We give our wives a questionnaire, and we have little interviews with our kids to get their input, too." In the dark, I heard him chuckle, and then he answered the first thought I had: "Yeah, right—if I hand a questionnaire to Marni and Hudson (Charlie wasn't born yet), they're going to laugh me out of the room: "C'mon Dad! We're filling out questions like we're in school?"

Then John started explaining the questionnaire:

"When was I a good husband this last year?"

"What have I done that you loved?

"What have I done that's bothered you, made you unhappy?"

(As John reeled off more questions, I thought, "Okay, Hudson would really get into this.")

"When was I a good dad?"

"What did I do this year that you really think was fantastic?"

"What did I do that you haven't liked so much that made you sad or frustrated?

"What are the dreams that you have for the next year?"

Off the top of his head, John ran through the list in the darkness, sounding sleepier and sleepier as he went along. I knew that was enough for one night, but the next day, between meetings, I pressed him for more. He shared with me the surveys the wives and kids fill out and some of the material they used for the first year's meeting. I have included all of this in the appendix for you, should you want to form your own covenant group.

At the time, I never suspected that the guy in the other bunk would make a lasting difference in my life.

Check out John's original list at the end of this chapter.
Challenge yourself and your family by pitching the questions
around the dinner table, and get ready for a lively evening.

In fact, John inspired me so much that I started a covenant group myself. How big of a difference has it made in our lives? We haven't missed a meeting in twenty-three years!

By the way, we're not talking about "goal setting" here. In my covenant group, we don't talk about goals; we talk about *intentions.* (Don't worry—goal setting has a place in a well-ordered life, but that's for the next chapter.) In a covenant group setting, we didn't want to use the word *goals* because in some years, however much you want to, that goal will still be beyond your reach.

For instance, imagine that you've made it your goal to find a more fulfilling job by the end of the year. Every year that you haven't changed careers, it's like having a neon sign blinking in your head that says, "Failed at that!"

But when you identify an *intention,* it means you're not afraid to examine it, go away for a while, think about it, and then come back again. During that time, maybe you decide to look into a whole new profession. Or maybe you enroll in a class that makes you more marketable. The point is, until you're ready, the intention is percolating and growing inside of you, gathering energy like a thundercloud right before the lightning strike.

Does it work? I have more examples ahead, but one intention that's skulked around the edges of my life for a number of years has been to write this book. Finally, the right time came. The proof is in your hands.

So, you might ask, *why* does it work? As John first explained it to me, the power of holding yourself accountable does this: It makes you stop and look at your life as a husband, a father, a friend, an employee. You look at your relationships, and you also look at what you want to accomplish—you're overweight, you're underweight, you're in debt, you're not in debt. You want to buy a boat; you want a cabin in the mountains. Not everything is material, either—some of our best intentions have to do with growing in our relationships with our families and with God. Maybe you want to repair a broken friendship, figure out how to have a less tense atmosphere at your office, or show more appreciation toward your wife.

John explained that the covenant group holds each person accountable for pursuing their intentions and for standing by them. No waffling, no backing out, no excuses. You stick to the game plan. Every year, you set your intentions for the next year. I realized that the difference I saw in John on our bunk night was that he was living by a compass that was calibrated to seek, year after year, what was good and true. The result was an integrity and confidence that just radiated from the guy.

Here's the craziest thing: As soon as my eyes were opened to the **power of intentional living, welcome changes started to multiply in my life.**

Before then, I had always been a pretty hard-charging guy. My attitude was basically, "If you can't keep up with me, kindly step out of my way." Don't get me wrong—I've always been a stable influence in my family (I'm pretty sure my wife Marni would tell you that, despite my faults, she's keeping me), but I had my blind spots.

All of a sudden, I was energized to make changes in my life, although I didn't necessarily expect other people to notice, at least right away. But I was back only a short while from that meeting in Colorado Springs when a guy I worked with as regional director suddenly stopped in the middle of our conversation and said in kind of a kidding way, "What is it with you? You aren't as rushed as before; you seem calmer ..."

A colleague had been begging me to give our work team the courtesy of at least a week's notice when a project was due (I tend to be a last-minute guy). But the next time she brought it up, I listened, and I followed through. She was amazed.

Then I heard through the grapevine that another colleague was asking people, "What's happened to Eric? He seems like a different guy. He's got more time to talk. I feel like he's not just stopping to *hear* me; he's really *considering* what I have to say."

Looking back, I didn't consciously change my behavior, at least right away. When I was dealing with people, I wasn't aware of pulling "good Sco" out of a hat like a magician. But over time, I was becoming a different guy. Listening to John, being introduced to the concept of the covenant group, then starting a covenant group—these were game changers, difference makers, in my life. And all it took was listening to the guy in the other bunk.

FLIGHT PLANS

Do you know someone in your life who changed everything for you?

Have you ever been told, "Thanks to you, I changed my life"?

What would it look like for you to live a more intentional life?

Who has been a game-changer for you? Take time to text, call, or write a note to them today.

Covenant Questions We Considered

As a follower:

- Am I being a good steward of the body God gave me?
- Am I nurturing my most important relationships?
- Am I stewarding my finances in a way that honors the Lord?
- Am I using my time wisely in pursuit of my particular purpose?
- Are my values reflected in the way I behave? Temptations? Struggles?

As a believer:

- Am I experiencing enough worship of my God?
- Am I more of a disciple of Jesus Christ than I was last year?
- Am I more of a servant of others, the church, and my family than last year?
- Am I bringing Christ into the center of my marriage? How? What?
- Am I experiencing true community with other believers on a regular basis?

FAIL TO PLAN, PLAN TO FAIL

'm a big coupon guy. I love deals. One came my way at the end of dinner at a fine restaurant in San Diego. I just didn't expect this deal to become a difference maker in my life.

It happened during a Young Life divisional leadership meeting. Dinner was done, and the senior vice president stood up to make an announcement. He had arranged an interesting half-price deal for us.

"Now, you're not required to do this," the executive leader told our group (there were about twenty of us). "But if any of you want to try the benefits of a life coach, I'll pay for half of your first year. Just see me after dinner."

To be honest, I felt deflated. If you're giving away stuff at half price, what about some half-price plane tickets to visit a Young Life group, say, in Hawaii or Latin America?

One thing I *didn't* need was somebody to run my life. I already had a great family, a fulfilling job, and meaningful friends. Most importantly, Jesus Christ was at the core of my life, and I was doing everything I could to introduce young people to Him. Why would I need a stranger to tell me how to improve all that, even at half price?

Then, my rebel side kicked in. I remember leaving the dinner saying to somebody, "I don't think a life coach would make any difference in my life at all. In fact, I so believe that it *won't* make a difference, I think I'm going to do it. It's only half price, so I'm going to take him up on it!"

That was in 2012. I signed up for the program and was connected with a guy named Dennis. I remember after our first meeting, I thought, "Hey, who's the coach here? It feels like I'm the one guiding this." I was looking for the point of it because I expected Dennis would begin by sending me off for a day, a whole eight hours, to answer questions like, "Where do you want to be in ten years?"

What I was about to learn was that wise planning doesn't happen by accident; it happens by design. But I had to learn this in stages.

Anyway, I had committed to the life coach idea, so, okay, I was game (at least until the half-price deal ran out). I was living in San Diego at the time, so naturally, the beach was the go-to place to ponder. With the sun-drenched Pacific rolling towards me as inspiration, I settled into a canvas chair, opened my journal, and started to address the questions my life coach Dennis had put to me.

To my surprise, the quiz started prying open my mind and heart in a way I didn't expect.

One of the first questions was, "Who do you want to be in ten years?" (Okay, this was interesting: The question wasn't "*Where* do you want to be?" It was, "*Who* do you want to be?")

Who do I want to be as a dad? *Who* do I want to be as a husband? The questions were starting to hit me directly in the gut. I wasn't being challenged geographically; I was being challenged *personally*. The questions were forcing me to probe deeper than "me-me-me" and my own wishful thinking; these questions were about the guy I saw in the mirror every day, and sometimes—let's face it, we all know this feeling—sometimes the guy I wanted to avoid.

So, I kept at it. Naturally, when I told people what I was doing, some of them wanted to know the difference between a covenant group and a life coach.

Here's the difference. You pray and get inspired with your covenant group. You *strategize* with your life coach. A covenant group is for sharing your big-picture hopes and yearnings with the other trusted members of the group. A life coach is a person who you meet with on the phone for thirty minutes every other week and hit three topics every single time. The goal is to move the ball forward—even if it's small yardage—when it comes to your financial future, your relationships, and your career.

It didn't take me long to put changes into action. I reached out to Dennis, a longtime friend and board member, and asked him to be my financial planner. I got life insurance for the first time in my life because, thanks to Dennis, it hit me for the first time that if I died … well, let's just say it would have been really traumatic for my wife and kids. I lost twenty-nine pounds and acquired two rental houses. Recently, I sold one of those rental houses for nearly three times what I paid for it. My son, Hudson, is living in the other rental house while he is going to college. From a seemingly small decision to manage my finances so that I could acquire rental houses, a great investment turned into a long-term blessing for our family because it meant that our son has a home to live in while he goes to college.

That goes to show how most decision-making radiates way beyond *yourself* and impacts everyone in your life.

Tons of things other things—big things, little things—started happening, but it wasn't magic; it was Dennis showing me how to make conscious decisions that would transform my life and my family's life in fulfilling ways.

Marni and I are going on date nights again. I regularly plan father-son trips with Hudson and Charlie—PGA Tour events, March Madness games, and even a fly-fishing trip in Colorado! Instead of shoe-horning a few days out of my meetings calendar, now we look forward to real family vacations that take us from New York City to Yosemite.

One of the pinnacle events was a father-son trip for all the families in our neighborhood. We rented a Young Life property in California, and I took nearly one hundred fathers and sons. It was epic, for sure, and it would not have happened without taking time to plan.

Even my relationship with God has changed for the better! Thanks to my life coach, I built quality time into my calendar to spend time with the Lord and, sometimes, I pull away to places that are very quiet and isolated. You could say I learned for myself what must have drawn Christ when He left the crowds and went "up a mountain to pray." I experienced that firsthand after spending a few days at a monastery in San Diego and, later, at Sacred Heart Retreat House outside of Denver. Those spiritual getaways enriched my soul.

Here's the thing. I always *wanted* those things to happen—deeper relationships with the family, more financial stability, regular vacations—but until I got a life coach, **I didn't have a plan for getting there.** Dennis held me accountable.

The drill was thirty minutes every other week. Some weeks, I looked forward to it, and some weeks, I felt like I was heading to a prison interrogation. Dennis always had questions for me—boom, boom, boom—did you get this done? How about that? Have you made that phone call yet? Gradually, I saw the wisdom of each one of these tasks, that each piece fit into a bigger picture that, like it or not, represented the full landscape of my life. But now I was getting somewhere! It made me realize what other, wiser guys than me had already recognized: "Sco, if you fail to plan, you might as well plan to fail."

Sometimes, I think about where I'd be without a plan. My date nights with Marni and all those family vacations would have been just another "shoulda, woulda, coulda." My financial situation compared to today? I don't even want to think about it. Dennis held me accountable, and that was the game changer for me.

Of course, the rules of the game were set long before I came along. The Bible tells us in Proverbs 24: 3-4 what outcomes we can expect if we work according to God's plan: *"Any enterprise is built by wise planning, becomes strong through common sense, and profits wonderfully by keeping abreast of the facts."*

Sounds like a life coach to me! Anyway, Dennis and I met regularly for about four years, and to this day, we check in with each other every couple of months. Dennis has become a friend, but first, he was a difference maker in my life. The money I spent, whatever it was, I made back tenfold.

What was that I said about life coaches?

Boy, was I glad to be wrong!

FLIGHT PLANS

- Have you made a plan for your life: Financial goals? Spiritual goals? Marriage goals? Health goals? Personal goals?
- Think about it: Who do YOU want to be ten years from now?
- Have you failed at anything? Looking back, can you think of a way you could have changed the outcome if you had only made a plan?

MAKE AN IMPACT. DO LESS.

Here's a secret every hard-working overachiever needs to learn: Let somebody else do it! You'll be amazed at what a difference it can make in your life.

I learned this one day just by looking out our front window.

What I saw was five guys weeding our yard. Except I didn't really see five guys weeding the yard—I saw a yard that looks like it belongs on *House and Garden* TV! Sure, everyone wants a good-looking yard. But unless you're really interested in maintaining your own yard, think about this: *It's usually when we give up control that our yards look this good.*

In other words, not everything we care about has to be directly in our power. In fact, sometimes things go better *because* we let go. Those five guys working on my front yard are doing a spectacular job—why would I want to change that? Is it pride that makes me want to say I did it myself? Or is it an arrogance that says, *"Nobody can do this better than I can?"*

So, do you want to star in your own one-person admiration society, or do you want to make a real impact in your life?

If your answer is to make an impact, start by shaking off the chorus in your head that goes, "Nobody can do this but me." Instead, learn the trick of *giving up* those details in your life, even risk the fact that other people might do it better.

I got turned on to this idea some years ago by a guy named Tim Ferris. He wrote a book called *The 4-Hour Work Week*, which became a bestseller because it promised what everybody wants—to work less and enjoy life more. Among his many tips and secrets was one that especially grabbed my attention. It was his belief in *the power of outsourcing.*

Outsourcing was not a word I used in my everyday vocabulary. But this concept by Ferris really caught my attention. How could I be doing many things at the same time—this was a capturing thought for me. Outsourcing for you might look way different than me, but examples for me at that time might have been a virtual assistant, a virtual phone number, the dictation service I started to use, and an occasional chef for an event. I was actually getting more done, and this was making a huge difference in my life.

Now, I'm not saying giving up control is easy. I'm an energetic kind of guy, and sometimes, to let other people take over work I feel I should be doing makes me feel really uneasy and out of control because: (1) I have to think ahead to give up control versus acting on the spur of the moment, and (2) I have the belief that, "I can do it better," which is just not true.

One of the first times I realized that outsourcing pays off was when I sent one hundred kids to Breakaway Lodge in Gearhart, Oregon. Young Life has since sold the camp, but for almost 50 years, it had given kids an amazing experience of learning about life from one of the planet's most spectacular locations. It's set near the spiny ridge of the Oregon coast, about four hundred yards from the Pacific Ocean, and it was known for its amazing access to all kinds of athletic activities, from hiking and beach tromping to kayaking on a near-by lake. Young Life took it over in 1969. In the Young Life world, Breakaway Lodge was known as "the best backyard anywhere."

Now, I was in charge of giving young kids that "backyard" ex-perience, and although I knew what I was doing, the responsibility weighed on me. I had been in Young Life since I was a teenager, and now that I was on the leadership side, I knew what I was getting into. Kids get sick, get stung, get lost, and get homesick. Prepare for anything! And here I was, scattering one hundred kids (along with the uneasy hopes of some two hundred anxious parents) away for the weekend into the wilderness, and I was not going to be there to solve whatever issues would surface. (And we know there will be issues!)

This was the weekend that was my growing weekend. What I mean by that is that we were growing with the number of weekend camps we would run, and I could not possibly go on all of them and maintain a life. So, this was my first time sending a camp and "outsourcing" to one of my capable younger staff. How could they get along without me?

It pretty much tormented me all weekend. I found myself think-ing: "How are they doing? How was the drive? How was the luggage unpacking?" I wonder how they handled the food preparation. Okay, now they're having breakfast ... now, they're on the beach doing the Olympics Games ... now, they're gathering for dinner and evening festivities... is anybody missing, hurt, or too sad to participate?

The first day they got home, I called my staff, cringing as I waited for the rundown of camp disasters, from bug bites to broken bones. Instead, I heard my staffer's cheerful voice and then the most hum-bling words of all.

"Oh, everything went great!" she said.

Oh, wait a minute—I was not missed! Of course, I was glad once I got over that sense that we all get sometimes—*wanting* to be missed. But when I thought about it more, I realized that this was actually a major moment in my quest to make a greater impact in my life. I had freed up significant time that I could devote to my family. I also realized I could take legitimate pride in something I did *not* do. Real leaders can train other leaders. Real leaders are not the center of everything. Real leaders are pouring into, investing in, and coaching up the next generation of leaders. Yes, this is outsourcing! One of the roadblocks to outsourcing is wanting to be in control or thinking that no one can do it as well as you. I had to laugh when I realized that I could give up power and control, and *camp happened*.

But here's the key. I had prepared well by putting excellent people in the breach so that when the time came, they knew what to do. Planning is critical to effective outsourcing. Once I learned that, I experienced a crazy freedom and release from the idea: "Well, if I don't do it, it won't get done right." Maybe it won't get done exactly as I would do it, but it *will* get done. Maybe even better.

Now for the kicker. When I realized I could outsource the camp weekend, this allowed me to focus on other key leadership opportunities that I sensed I wanted our area to grow in. Outsourcing may be a drab and colorless word, but without it, I would not have been able to offer support and comfort to the people I loved and who needed me most. It's been a huge difference maker in my life.

As for the campers (brace yourself, Sco), they did amazingly fine without me.

It was at Crooked Creek Camp that I learned the power of out-sourcing 350 times faster than I would have any other way.

For staff, prepping for this week-long camp in Fraser, Colorado, is like bracing for a "Category 5" hurricane. Some 350 kids swarm into the vast spread (one of the largest Young Life camps anywhere), and they are all blazing with abundant energy, just waiting to be inspired and entertained. Bracing for their arrival is the forty-member work crew, mostly high school kids who clean the tables, serve the food, do the dishes, and clean the toilets. Then there's the college summer staff, *another* forty workers strong. By the way, the work crew and summer staff are all volunteers who pay to get to do this work at the Young Life camp for a month. They keep the discipline and the scores for all the sports like the zipline, the rope course, the horse rides, the mountain bike experience, and the ridge runner course. Whatever is on the schedule, the summer staff has to be ready for it.

On the big finale night, this indispensable staff makes magic by transitioning the basketball court into a carnival scene, with lights and music, a square dance floor, and cotton candy blooming up out of nowhere. All of this ends with kids getting to experience the swimming pool open for a night swim, as well as the camp open for basketball, a snack shop, and just hanging around with friends.

Oh, one more complication: it's also opera night. The la-de-da name refers to the fact that the opera features a pretty crazy thirty-five minutes of drama and singing. The kids love it because it's an interactive play featuring a nefarious villain who is attempting to take over a town of good people.

It's entertaining, but the opera has a secret, practical purpose. The evening is on a schedule tighter than an acrobat's highwire, and the opera is actually a 35-minute stall tactic. Behind the scenes, the staff is scurrying around to set up the rest of the evening.

That's pretty good planning, but there's the catch: It's impossible to cram in the finale dinner (and cleanup) for 350 kids, set up for the carnival, a square dance, a night swim in the pool, *and* an opera, and do it so smoothly that every worker can participate equally in the magical finale.

In some years past, the task of putting on the event—but not being able to enjoy it—weighed so heavy on the workers that what should have been the happiest of evenings for the staff turned into a grim slog. The kitchen staff went about their dreary, assigned duties of dishwashing, spaghetti-plate-cleaning, and setting up scenery without any hope of taking part in the grand celebration they helped create.

To me, this felt like an outsourcing moment, if there ever was one. I knew it was wrong that the most important people involved in that week—the staff—were being scattered and minimalized by tasks that could be outsourced more effectively among the whole team. It wasn't right that some of them would be robbed of the evening's memories because they were stuck scraping spaghetti off plates! So, at a meeting before the grand finale evening, I told the staff and crew, "Don't worry about cleaning the dining hall. I want everybody to see the opera. I also need some of you to help with the square dance, and I need some help at the pool because we go right from the carnival to the square dance, and anybody can go into the pool with their clothes on. We will need people standing around the pool to watch for extra safety."

As I assigned people to specific tasks, I could see everybody's spirits lift. They were no longer random cogs in a wheel but individuals with responsibilities. Everybody was getting a chance to participate in the spirit of the evening.

Then, when the opera was over and the evening was coming to a close, *everybody* pitched in to tackle the hundreds of spaghetti-smeared plates, greasy glasses, and crusty knives and forks. With all hands on deck—about eighty workers in all—the result was unbelievable. We finished cleanup in close to fifteen minutes, what would have taken the work crew two hours! Everybody had a meaningful task, and that made the work go even faster. Maybe that's not possible at every meal, but you can see the powerful, multiplying effects when jobs are outsourced. Now *that's* a difference maker!

By now, you can tell I really believe in outsourcing as a way to make a difference in your life. If you have big dreams and you want to accomplish a lot of things, *you're going to have to give up things.*

Maybe I grabbed this idea at first from a book, but I learned the wisdom of it from a good friend of mine.

Ben Crane is a five-time PGA winner, with twenty years as a PGA tour pro and personal priorities that are as fresh and clear as rainwater. Here's how he describes himself on his social media accounts: "Jesus Follower, Husband/Father, Pro Golfer." Hard to argue with a list like that! He's among the top golfers in the world, but more than some players, he seems to attract media attention, maybe because, despite his awesome talents, he's had his share of tour setbacks, from physical ailments like a bad back to bad luck on the greens. But he never stops fighting. People, and the media, seem drawn to that. After all, not every golfer gets a long, admiring write-up in *Golf Digest* for making a "career detour." Likewise, few golfers are known for their quotable lines, but Ben is known for saying more than once: "I think sometimes it's great to face your fears."

Besides being my friend and a fellow Oregonian, Ben was one of the first people to build a team around himself. Talk about understanding the power of outsourcing!

Ben knows he can't do everything himself, so he builds a team. He has a mental coach and a physical coach—the first to help manage the pressures of the tour and the second to keep the pressures off his back, literally. He also has a short game coach, a manager, a financial guy, and a nutritionist, about seven coaches in all. And he has a life coach. Ben has learned, while pulling this team together a number of times, that for him to accomplish as much as he can in his life, he needs to have help to do it. I had the chance to help Ben with a life plan and some other aspects, mostly of things off the golf course versus on.

Sometimes, I wonder who's coaching whom because Ben has taught me so much about how to make an impact in life. Later, I'll say more about Ben and about the lessons I've learned from the golf course that have nothing to do with golf.

FLIGHT PLANS

What's the number one task weighing on your mind? If you could outsource that task to someone else, who would it be?

_____

_____

What are your five deepest time traps? (Tasks/responsibilities that take you away from the things you really want to do)

_____

_____

Ask the most focused people you know how *they* outsource. What can you learn from their answers?

_____

_____

BE FAT
BUT NOT WHAT YOU THINK

My whole life, it seems I've been on the lookout for somebody. I've been looking for volunteers, student leaders, or a basketball player that I can coach. Now, a little later in life, I'm still looking for people, this time to hire them as area directors, regional directors, or development directors for a city, town, or project.

The kind of person I'm looking for is very specific, and I pretty much know them when I meet them. I'm looking for people who rise above the ordinary—like Sequoia trees. They are tall, deep, and unmovable. It's not a physical thing; it's in their spirit. You can count on them.

They're FAT, too: *Faithful, Available, Teachable.*

When a FAT person gets involved, they get stuff done. More often than not, they are also unforgettable.

When you understand the kind of people I'm talking about, I'm pretty sure you'll think to yourself, "Hey, I know somebody like that!" Or maybe you think, "I was really hurt by that person, and now I know why. When I needed them most, they were *not available.*"

I believe that the quality of being FAT—or not—runs like an undercurrent through all our lives. Every person we meet, live with, or remember, is on a FAT scale. On the flip side, so are we! If we want to truly make an impact in life, we need to get on the FAT scale to see how we stack up. I hope these stories help you identify your own universe of FAT people, and maybe, somewhere in these stories, you will see yourself.

Do you know that feeling of putting out an invitation and never hearing back? One time, I was organizing a big Young Life breakfast, and I was a little anxious about it. Competing with the croissants and coffee were some major agenda items.

In the middle of planning, I got a call from a good friend, Richard King Brown. Richard is a native New Yorker who went to high school in Colorado Springs and, from there, fell permanently in love with the West. He's been here ever since, but he never lost that brisk, no-nonsense, big-city vibe that drives him to get things done and with impressive style. So that morning, I had to smile when I heard his voice.

"What time do you start? I want to be there!"

"Are you sure, Richard?" I said. "It starts at 6:30, and you live on the other side of town."

"No, I really want to come. I want to see this thing. I'll see you at 6:18."

(Not 6 o'clock, or 6:15, or "a few minutes before you start." No, *6:18.)*

What time do you think Richard King Brown walked through the door? 6:18.

This was Richard's character in action, but I had seen it many times before. *If Richard says he's going to do something, he does it.* We're losing people like this in our culture! Instead, we've become resigned to a huge number of people in our lives who love to cancel, or who show up late, or not at all. The word *faithful* is not in their vocabulary or mindset. But so many qualities are bound up in that one word—qualities like integrity, commitment, courage—though sometimes they masquerade in something as simple as being some-where exactly when you promised to be.

If you want to make an impact in life (and even be remembered for it), commit to your own version of 6:18. It's pretty simple, and yet not simple at all. "Do what you say you are going to do." Do it. Be the kind of person that follows through. It may not be easy to follow through, pending what you said you would do, but it will be rewarding to be the person whose "Yes" was a "Yes." It's a good way to start getting FAT.

Now for a short wedding story. It happened to be *my* wedding. I had six groomsmen and a solid bench of good friends as readers and ushers. Then, there were a lot of other good guys who came just to support me for that three-day run-up to the big day. We had a day of golf, then the rehearsal day, and then the happiest day of all, the day I married Marni. It was a memorable weekend, with lots of details woven all through the happiness.

One of the friends who supported me from point A to point B and points beyond was a guy named John Heywood. At that time, he was just out of college and starting his first job as a copier salesman.

Now, why do I remember John these many years later? It's because John was FAT. Everywhere I turned for that three-day run-up to marrying Marni, John seemed to be at my side. At one point, I realized I lost my cummerbund. "I got it," John said. All weekend, whatever was missing, expected, or had to be done, John's answer was, "I got it." He was *available*.

The quality that John showed at my wedding wasn't a one-wedding phenomenon, either. He went on to be one of those special guys who built a great career and found much success in his field. I'm sure no small part of his success was his ability *to be there* when he was needed most.

John's quiet but towering presence at my wedding always makes me think of the Sequoia tree. He's the kind of person I'm always looking for to fill a job or a critical task. Obviously, his success proved that other people in authority saw in John what I experienced on that milestone day in my life. He is a FAT guy, through and through, and there's one formerly nervous groom out there who has never forgotten it. How about you? Does it make you think of people in your life that, when they say, "Got it," you know they do? How about you? Are you a "got it" person, and you create in others a sense of full trust—they know that you will do what you say, and when you say you will do it?

You might wonder why being *teachable* can make you FAT. This a lesson I had to learn myself. At the time, I was the regional director with twenty-six area directors working for me, and I was keenly aware that their livelihood depended on my evaluation. Their salary was directly tied to their performance, and to get a full paycheck, they had to increase their skills at fundraising in a yearly budget that, over time, always goes up, not down.

This particular year, we were holding our staff retreat in 115-degree Palm Springs, where very nice hotels are cheap to come by when it's sweltering outside. Young Life is serious about its mission, but when the day's work is over, it also knows how to treat its staff to a good party, and this one was in full swing. In the middle of it, one of the area directors came up and asked if he could talk to me privately.

As we walked into the lobby, I could tell he was nervous. I knew he was director of one of our toughest and challenged areas, and his budget wasn't growing; in fact, it was going into deficit, and that meant his paycheck was, as we say in Young Life, on "short pay." In other words, he was taking a pay cut. But that's the salary structure at Young Life, and everybody knows it before they respond to the call to be a part of the mission. The young man took a long breath, and then he said, "You know that I'm on short pay, and I have a wife and four kids?" I nodded. Then he said, "You know you've never asked what this is like for me? You've never asked how I'm doing during this hard time?"

At that moment, in my mind, I kind of staggered backward as if I had been punched. Obviously, I had missed something that was very important to this young man, and it cut me to the core not to have seen it. But it didn't mean I wasn't aware. *Of course,* I knew it was hard for him! I hadn't asked him about it because I knew he was going through something awful. What else was there to say?

As I tried to explain that, the young man broke in. "No, no, you need to *talk to people* in these moments. You need to ask, 'How are you doing? How can I help? What's this like for you?' Do you know what it's like for me, sitting in this fancy hotel suite with a king-size bed and air conditioning when my family is in my brother's apartment, sleeping on the floor in 100-degree heat? Well, I can't do this anymore. I'm leaving."

Well, this was one retreat where the boss learned more than his staff. First of all, I learned that even when you know somebody's going through something really hard, it's okay to ask how hard it is. In a way, it's a matter of being *faithful, available, and teachable* all at the same time. You need to stay faithful to people by reassuring them that you have their back. You need to show you're available. And sometimes, you need to change. Like I did.

My friend Jeremy left, and I walked into our staff meeting with my tail between my legs. I felt awful, and so I shared with my staff my learnings, my mistakes, and my shortcomings as a leader. I remember people really commenting on how much they appreciated hearing not about a success but rather a failure. One person came up during the next break and asked what the shortfall was—and I said it was about $5,000. They said, "Well, here you go." And this Young Life staff person handed over a personal check. Others heard about this gift and wanted to match it. So, in a matter of moments, really, this area went from down to up $5,000! All of this took place because of being teachable.

When I was 19 years old and still a staff rookie at Young Life, I got a piece of advice from the guy who trained me that has stuck with me forever.

"Whatever you do," he said, "weddings and funerals, *show up*." Later, he added, "Hospitals, too."

I have followed his advice. No matter how busy I've been on any given day, no matter how much I've gritted my teeth over having to change plans or redo my schedule, I've never regretted the times I've stopped everything to be with people in a time of crisis.

Years ago, a kid named Pat, just a sophomore in high school, went snowboarding and broke his neck. He was paralyzed from the neck down. I was a young staffer then, and I remember thinking, "No, I don't want to go to the hospital. I don't want to see him like that." But Rob, another staff member, said, "C'mon, we're gonna go." We walked into his room and saw this really good athlete flat on his back, immovable, *forever*. It was hard to take. I wanted to leave. And yet, when you show up and know that hard is always hard, there are lessons to learn. We hung out with Pat and talked about normal life. We told him what was going on with all of his buddies, we talked about what was next for him in his rehab, and we did what kids like to do—joked and laughed, which seemed impossible. On our way out, Pat had a request. "Hey, before you guys leave, would you give me a hug?"

Well, you can't really hug someone in that state. You can only go up and press your chest on their chest and put your cheek on their cheek. So, that's what I did. I went up and put my chest on Pat's chest and my cheek on his cheek, and I said, "We love you. We're praying for you." And I meant it. Then my friend Rob went up and did the same thing.

We were ready to leave, and Pat said, "Could I get one more?" So, we both hugged him a second time. I had gone from dreading the visit to being glad just to touch his chest and cheek!

Only when I was much older and hopefully a little bit wiser did I realize what that visit meant, both to Pat and to two awkward young men who, at the start of the visit, would have given almost anything to be somewhere else that day. But no, not at the end! At the end of that visit, I realized that we need to reach out to people because nine times out of ten, they're waiting for us to do it. We may not know what to say. We may not know what to do or to bring, and it doesn't matter. Just be there. Be available. Be FAT. Do *something*.

Here's one more story about showing up. This one touched me in a way I can't explain because it was at the funeral of my brother, Paul. Four years ago, he died suddenly and traumatically of an aortic dissection. Paul was an amazing guy. A couple of things stand out about that sad time. One was that when I got to the funeral, I saw two people there who didn't even know him. They flew into town to be with me. Now, that's being faithful and available.

The other thing is that I got seventy-five sympathy cards, and I appreciated them all, but one card from a good friend stood out. It was a simple card with a one-word message: *Shit.*

A little raw, maybe, but the message said everything that had to be said about that miserable time. So often, we miss opportunities in life to make an impact because we're so worried about being perfect, about saying just the right thing. Or we fear we won't say enough, or we'll offend somebody. It doesn't matter. Just reach out. Maybe one word is enough.

FLIGHT PLANS

How do you stack up as a FAT person? Rate yourself on a scale of 1 to 10:

Faithful_____

Available_____

Teachable_____

On a scale of 1 to 10, how much can you be counted on to be there for the people in your life?_____

Family_____

Friends_____

Colleagues_____

Who is the one person in your life you'd most like to reveal your FAT side to (show more availability and constancy)?_____

What are three roadblocks that you believe keep you from being as available as you could be?_____

_____

How about two ideas for eliminating those roadblocks?_____

_____

_____

THE LUMP OF STEEL

I f you're a kid whose dream is to play serious basketball, you couldn't do better than to spend a week at Cascade Sports Camp, about an hour outside of Portland, Oregon. Not only are the surroundings spectacular—in the foothills of the Cascade Mountains—but the camp has a pedigree that shimmers with Oregon sports royalty.

For a number of years, I was a summer counselor at Sports Camp and was privileged to be there in the era of its founder, Barry Adams, a legend in Oregon sports. Barry coached high school sports for forty years and held the official title of one of the "Most Winningest Coach in Oregon High School History," with 656 wins as a high school coach. No one was surprised when he was inducted into the Oregon Sports Hall of Fame. On his own, he founded Sports Camp and created positive, lifelong memories for 56,000 young camp graduates who came for a week of testing their sports skills and challenging themselves as young men.

Barry Adams—an amazing guy! But it's Barry's number two guy I want to tell you about.

When you saw Lytle Cowell for the first time, you might be inclined to call security. He just didn't look like he belonged in a camp for athletes. He looked like one of those Tasmanian Devils—kind of squat and hunched but powerful-looking. His upper body was huge, but not necessarily fat, as if somebody took a straw, poked it in his side, and just blew him up. From the waist down, it was as if nothing was there. His legs were like toothpicks.

All of this goes to prove that looks aren't everything because Coach Cowell radiated personality. He embodied the culture of the camp. Every kid wanted to be on Lytle's team. He had a way of motivating each kid to be the best basketball player he could be, even though it was clear just by looking at him that Lytle Cowell never was, and never would be, a basketball player himself.

Most of all, he was a great storyteller and motivator. I'm telling you, out there in the world, grown men are measuring their lives by a story they heard first from Coach Cowell.

On Tuesday nights during sports week, Coach Cowell taught the camp kids the science of how to shoot a basketball. It was fascinating to watch him. His hands would pass over the ball like he had been born with it cupped there, in his hands, since birth. He knew a basketball that well. The kids would hang on to his every move. He'd stroke the ball, roll it through his fingers, weigh it in his palms. Every one of Coach Cowell's movements said something about the science of shooting a basket. He'd explain where to put your feet and how to balance, and he did it so carefully and gracefully it was like watching somebody glide across a dance floor.

Finally, after he'd explained the science of how to shoot a basketball, Lytle would advance to the hoop for the shot. Everybody sat forward a little, eyes glued to Coach. You'd swear he was about to let the ball go—being a basketball player myself, I know it's really hard to be on a basketball court, holding a ball in your hands and not go for a shot—but when Coach Cowell held the ball in his hands, everything seemed to revert to slow motion.

In fact, at least not to my knowledge, no one ever saw Coach Cowell actually shoot a basketball.

It was a special magic he had, making things seem to appear and then disappear right before your eyes! The kids were mesmerized. As they drifted off to sleep that night, I bet they saw Coach dunk the ball a million times in their dreams. Even though it never happened in real life, that's how much they believed in him and learned from him.

Anyway, the week went by fast, and at the end of it, the kids were exhausted. The staff knew it, so they made the final night really memorable: a big, grand finale presentation with platters of gooey cinnamon rolls to keep everybody awake, and the staff telling camp stories to make everybody laugh.

The night always ended on a crescendo, which was when Lytle stood up to give a talk. It was the same talk every single summer, so if you went to camp every year, you knew what was coming. You could see veteran kids grinning and elbowing each other, *"Here it comes, here it comes."* Trust me, nobody was complaining.

The moment came, and Coach Cowell stood up at the front of 112 kids and all the coaches and staff. Just like he never actually took a hoop shot, Coach Cowell didn't connect directly with people. He never looked anybody in the eye. But those of us who knew him knew this was from shyness, not shiftiness. On the last night of camp, he'd look up into the sky, then he'd look far away, and then he would launch into the story of "The Lump of Steel."

Here is my recollection of that story.

"Three men were trudging down a road when they came upon a lump of steel tossed off in the underbrush. It was ugly, misshapen, and had nothing going for it. The guys decide to take the lump of steel to an ironworker and have it broken into three pieces so each could have a chunk.

"After the lump of steel is divided up, the first guy looks at his lump of steel and says, 'Say! I can do something with this! I can make thousands of sewing needles and sell them all.' And he does. He sells a thousand sewing needles for $5 each and makes $5,000.

"The second guy looks at his lump of steel and announces, 'I've always wanted to make a very unusual piece of furniture, a one-of-a-kind chair, and this lump of steel would make very unique chair legs. Somebody will pay big money for that chair!' So, he does and sells his masterpiece chair for $10,000.

"The third guy has connections in the space industry, so he takes his lump of steel to his expert and discovers something about it that would make a great component for the toilet seat on the space shuttle. He sells his lump of steel to NASA for $200,000."

As you can tell, Coach Cowell used a lot of poetic license in his storytelling. On the chance the kids found some of his examples a little far-fetched, every few weeks, he changed up the details of the "Lump of Steel" story. Nobody minded, even the ones who had heard the story a million times.

But the "three guys" part of the story wasn't the end of it, not by a long shot. Coach Cowell was just getting started.

Coach paused for effect, and the kids sat there waiting (and probably wondering what a toilet seat on the shuttle actually *does* look like). Then, Coach Cowell leaned forward, and you could see the

40

kids shiver a little in excitement. His voice rose. He came as close to looking anybody in the eye as he ever would.

"So, what are you going to do with your lump of steel?"

You could hear crickets sawing outside. It was *that* quiet. Every eye was laser-beamed on Coach Cowell. He was painting a picture. You could see it take shape, kind of like the picture he painted to explain the science of shooting a basketball—the ball cupped in his hands, almost begging to be thrown—when you could almost see Michael Jordan or Shaquille O'Neill stepping out of the shadows and waiting for the Coach make his shot.

"So, what are you going to do with your lump of steel?"

This time, Coach Cowell was painting a picture to challenge the kids about their future. "When you're sitting in front of the TV and watching the Warriors or the Lakers," he said, "what are you thinking about? Are you thinking about what it takes a Lebron James or a Stephen Curry to get where they are? Do you see that they started with *a lump of steel* like everybody else, and the only difference between them and the guy still sitting on his couch is that they made something out of it?"

I was in the back of the room, watching the Coach weave his magic. He extended the lesson to include family relationships and going off to college, but he'd always bring it back to basketball. And I would watch these 12-, 14-, 15-year-old kids straighten up and shake their shoulders. They weren't exhausted anymore. When they left the hall that night, they were all like, "Well, *okay.*" Somebody had told them what to do if they wanted to make something of themselves.

That night, after Coach Cowell's talk, the whole mood was different. (Sleep? What's that?) The kids stayed up practically till dawn, shooting baskets and doing pushups. Everybody was motivated to dream big. Really big.

Coach Cowell was that kind of difference maker. Not just for the kids, either—I learned a lot during those summers, and I bet the other adults did, too. His lesson was to shoot for the stars. If you don't hit one, that's okay. Try again.

At Sports Camp, we all learned to look *up*—because of Lytle Cowell. Talk about a Sequoia tree! He may have been disguised as a Tasmanian devil, and as the assistant coach, he was far down on the list for the corner office, but he stood tall in all our eyes.

If only more kids had a chance to meet him. About twenty-five years ago, Lytle, who was still a young man, died of a massive heart attack. Probably six hundred people came to his funeral.

When I think about Coach Cowell and the "The Lump of Steel," sometimes I wonder: Was Lytle telling his own story? Was he the kid sitting on the couch, watching the stars of the NBA on TV and realizing that with his body, his toothpick legs, he would never be one of them?

But he could be *something*. I bet Lytle told himself that. He took the lump of steel that God gave him and turned himself into the coach every kid wanted to have and the kind of man every kid wanted to be.

This I learned from Lytle, which I will take with me forever in hopes of being just a little more like him. Lytle wanted to be a difference maker. He chose a career to make a difference, and this is why he taught. Lytle wanted to coach, knowing that the life lessons he could teach kids in athletics were too numerous to count. And Lytle, in the summer, coached thousands of kids and tried to drive home to point—dream, work hard, and nothing is out of your reach. We have all been given the same "lump of steel." Now, what you do with it is up to you!

FLIGHT PLANS

Can you think of a person in your life whom you discounted at first? Shrugged them off because they didn't seem like they had it all together?

What changed your mind about them?

Think back—what in your life counts as "lumps of steel?" What have you done with these seemingly useless circumstances in your life?

Can you think of someone who needs your help to identify *their* lump of steel? (A student in class? One of your own children?) How can you help them make something out of a seemingly hopeless situation?

BUILT TO FLY

This story is closest to my mind and heart, so it's fitting that it begins at the address of my childhood home, 450 Holmes Court, Salem, Oregon.

Specifically, it begins in our garage. In the garage, my dad was building his dream machine. But it was a very different dream machine than most dads' dream machines.

His dream flew.

In 1968, when I was about four years old, my dad started to build Starduster Too, a vintage-style bi-plane with an open cockpit and seating for two. Since it was an open cockpit, both the pilot in the back and the passenger in the front would wear leather helmets with built-in headphones and goggles.

It took my dad four years to build Starduster Too. To our family, it seemed perfectly normal (and to a kid like me, perfectly wonderful) to see massive wings drying on our living room floor. Later, I learned that Mom didn't always find it so wonderful to be stepping over wings and propeller bits to get to the sofa, but she was always a good sport. It never had to be said outright—everybody knew this was a family enterprise, and we were there to help Dad in any way we could. I can't count the times I was beckoned out to the garage to hold some vital piece of machinery while Dad struggled to find its

45

proper slot on the Starduster's flank! Other times, he'd call us out to the garage just to announce he had completed another phase, and I remember when he did that, his face was always beaming.

For me, Starduster Too was more than wings and engine parts; for me, watching my dad at work was watching a work of art being made from scratch. Later, when I was older, I made the connection with our Father in Heaven, who has built each of us "from scratch," so to speak, and built us with meticulous care and love. And even if, at times, we break or our dreams don't work out the first time, God will find a way to make it right because He designed each of us to soar.

As for my dad, he didn't just love the dream—he loved *building* the dream and guiding it to reality. But he wasn't a "pie-in-the-sky" dreamer; he was a doer. He hung a picture above the workbench that chronicled each phase of Starduster Too's creation, and he loved to point out the picture to neighbors and friends when they'd stop by to see how far along he had come since the last time they were there.

Meanwhile, I was a normal, happy kid who rode my bike, played basketball, went to school, and had friends whose dads did things, too. Three of their dads golfed, one played tennis, one never missed an Oregon State Beaver game, and one was really into yard work. And my dad was building an airplane.

Early in life, because of my dad's dream, I learned one sad thing about human nature—people who aspire to do great things attract scoffers. I know my dad did. He had to put up with a lot of people who said, "It'll never fly." On the other hand, my friends were respectful and excited. They liked coming over and sitting in the un-finished frame. Maybe because we were young, we could understand a dream better than older people who had become cynical about life. That was a great thing about my dad—he was never cynical. He had a boyish energy and eagerness that never left him, and it made him completely confident in the future of Starduster Too. He knew it was going to fly. But Dad was also very patient, and he went through all the building steps methodically, never getting too excited or ahead of himself.

That drove me nuts. I was not anywhere near as patient as my dad.

For me, total satisfaction didn't come until the fabric was smoothed on and you could see that you were looking at an actual airplane. I was downright ecstatic when the plane was finally painted, and I could watch Dad peel off the masking tape to reveal the stars, the plane's call numbers, and the stripes up and down the plane's flanks. That's when I knew it was going to work out. Of course, Dad knew long before me. If you tell me that sounds a lot like praying to our Heavenly Father and then having to wait a long time for answers, well, I'm right there with you. It happened in our garage as I watched my dad's wise plan unfold with just the right timing.

The day finally came when Dad pulled the plane out of the ga-rage, assembled the wings, and proceeded to start the plane's engine. It was such a moment—I cannot express how proud I was! First, to see the plane virtually finished, not in the garage anymore, but out there, on the street, for everyone to see! Then, to watch the faces of my friends when the engine roared—priceless. Finally, to see my dad being patted on the back by all his neighbors (even by the scoffers) and being handed a glass of champagne. It was a day of celebration.

So, the plane was finished and ready to be taken to the airport. It had the words "Experimental" written near where the pilot sits. That meant no passengers could fly in Starduster Too until it had been flown fifty hours. In plane years, that's a long, long time. But there was a prize at the end of it—Dad promised that when the fifty hours were up, I would fly with him first.

Every time I watched him take off, first trundling down the runway and then—miracle!—lifting off from planet Earth, I imagined the day I would be in that front seat too, wearing helmet and goggles, scrunched down in the co-pilot seat, right behind my dad.

But you know what was almost as thrilling? To be on solid ground and to look up and see Dad flying over 450 Holmes Court at about 1,000 feet. He would dip the wings as he flew by, and I could imagine him, his head swathed in the old fashioned, daredevilish, Red Baron leather cap, and waving to us as he streaked by.

On a brisk and sunny March day in 1973, my dad headed out to the airport for a regular Saturday flight. He had only about twelve hours to go to make the fifty, and it was spectacular flying weather—cool and windless. I was in the street with all the fellas (there were always a handful of us), and we were doing what third graders do on their bikes, practicing wheelies and jumps.

Should I go with Dad to the airport? I always felt a tug whenever my dad left for a date with Starduster Too—should I go with him, or stay at home? I usually went with him, but for some reason, this day I didn't.

Not too long after he left, I remember hearing the plane off in the distance. I knew it was my dad's plane the way a mother knows her baby's cry.

Sure enough, off in the distance, just above the horizon, you could see the silhouette of a biplane coming directly toward our street. Down went the bikes. "Here he comes! Here he comes!" We were all yelling (me, maybe, most of all). If I had to scrape some tears off my face at the same time, well, I'd never admit it, back then anyway. All I know is that there was something reverent about watching this graceful machine—brought to life in our garage!—and knowing it all happened because of my dad. Now he was barnstorming down our street and close enough to see all the neighbor kids waving and running after his plane. High above us, how he must have been grinning at the sight!

Then the fly-over was over. Once Dad flew by and the sound of Starduster Too faded away, we groundlings kind of looked at each other, marveling at what we had just seen, and then we did a few more wheelies on our bikes. Somehow, those wheelies didn't seem so exciting anymore, not after watching Mr. Scofield buzz the street in his new airplane.

Pretty soon, I was racing to pursue another little-kid interest— rooting out a cache of graham crackers, peanut butter, and a tall glass of milk. I was in our kitchen doing just that when I heard the phone ring. I raced to pick up our second phone because my mother picked up the main phone first.

"Yes, this is Bob Scofield's wife," I heard her say.

The pause that followed didn't sound good. I got scared even before I knew why. I gripped the handle of the phone I was holding.

"Well, Mrs. Scofield, there has been an accident. I am sorry to say that your husband has crashed his airplane ..."

I dropped my phone and ran out the front door with no shoes—just my socks. I didn't know what to do except to run in the direction of my dad's flight path. I was running as fast as I ever had—maybe faster—and all I could think about was my dad dipping the wings overhead and then disappearing into the distance, leaving us behind.

My flight path took me down the end of the street and through a stretch of woodland forest that eventually spilled out onto a busy street in Salem, Oregon.

There, I stopped. I was in the parking lot of Bob's Hamburgers in my dirty socks, crying, and convinced my dad was dead. I could not get the image out of my mind of his last flight over the street, or his captivating smile, or even his flight suit that he wore to the airport with his name stitched on his chest in neat cursive writing, "Bob."

I just stood there, crying, when all of a sudden, a young guy in a Trans Am pulled up next to me and asked what was wrong. "My dad was in a plane crash," I said. "I don't know if he is alive or dead, but I just want to find him."

"Get in, kid." At the moment, which was harder to believe—that I got into a stranger's car or that my dad crashed an airplane? It didn't matter. We drove in and out of every street that led to the airport in search of a blocked-off street, an ambulance, a fire truck, something that would prove that I was telling the truth. We were getting dangerously close to the airport and, specifically, very nearly running out of neighborhoods to look.

Then we passed Ewald Park, and I could see that the street beyond the park was blocked off. My newfound friend pulled me up to the barricades, and I got out.

Still in my socks, I just bolted through the barricades and ran toward all the activity. There were police cars, ambulances, fire trucks, flatbed trucks, hundreds of people! I was too short to see, but I was relentless— I wormed my way through the crowds and finally broke through the final line of defense that kept me from seeing a crushing sight.

In front of me was Starduster Too. An hour before, we had cheered her proud passage across the sky—now she was an ugly, twisted wreck. Even worse than looking at her crumpled frame were the mutterings I could hear behind me.

"What was he thinking?"

"That plane is ruined."

"No one can survive that."

"My god, that is mangled."

Hearing the comments made me more desperate. Where was my dad? Was he okay? But the wreckage was telling the story, and that was all I needed to know. My dad was dead.

Through tears, I began to scream, "Dad! That's my dad! Dad, where are you?"

My dad's mangled plane was sitting neatly between two stately suburban homes in an exclusive South Salem neighborhood. Later, people would say that Bob Scofield made an amazing and heroic landing. There were kids in the park nearby, there were kids playing on the street, and there were kids in the front yards. My dad landed Stardust Too in the one spot that was safe from all the children—between two houses.

My dad's emergency landing became legendary. Years later, I would coach a kid who lived in one of those stately homes that flanked my dad's wrecked plane. The family often told the story of how the kid, then just a baby, was sleeping in his crib no more than five feet from the plane's tail.

But where was my dad?

As I stood there, taking in the wreckage, totally heartbroken, I saw a sight that will never leave me as long as I live. My dad stepped out of the garage of one of these homes and stood in the yard, surveying the wreckage. He looked weary and heartbroken, too. But what was important was that he was *there*. I tore across the lawn and literally took flight as I hurled my whole body into his chest. To have my arms around him, to bury my face in his flight suit, to drink in the faint smell of Old Spice from his morning shave—pure joy. My dad was *alive!*

122nd Year 8 Sections - 92 Pages Salem, Oregon, Sunday, March 4, 1973 Price 15c No. 342

Safe Landing Bob Scofield, Salem, walks away from the wreckage of his home built biplane Saturday afternoon following a crash landing between two houses in a residential area. The plane's engine failed as Scofield was approaching McNary Field and Scofield was forced to land between two houses less than 30 feet apart. The right wing of the plane struck the garage and patio of the James Adams residence, 1456 Ewald Ave. SE, and the tail struck the side of the Carl Ferris residence, 1476 Ewald. Scofield walked away without a scratch and there were no injuries to occupants of either house. (Statesman photo by Ron Cooper)

My dad's plane after the crash

"I love you, dad," I said.

"I love you too, son," my dad said, and I could tell from his voice that he was completely spent and exhausted, but that holding me in his arms was not just comforting me; it was comforting him, too. I never wanted to let go of him. I think he felt the same.

I was sure my dad had died. The dread and the permanence of death—especially of someone I loved so deeply, made a lifelong impression on me. Then to have life restored, to be wrapped in my dad's arms, left me with a joy that is unexplainable.

As I got older, I started to make a deeper connection. When all seems lost, when we look around us and see nothing but the wreckage of our hopes and dreams, we need to remember that Christ allowed Himself to become a complete wreckage on the cross, only to rise again on the third day.

I thought of Christ building his ministry—like my dad building his airplane—methodically and purposefully over time. He was not going to reveal His plan to the world until He was ready.

I thought about my role, too. I was like Peter, waiting for the chance to be in the front seat with his leader. Peter had watched Jesus build his ministry and reputation, and now it was time to fly. Instead, Peter watches Jesus go to the cross. Wait a minute—that's not part of the plan!

The loss of my dad's dream, Stardust Too, wasn't part of our plan, either. It all began to hit me later that night. My parents urged me to go to a long-planned school carnival, to have some fun, and to try to forget the traumatic day. So, I went. I did the cake walk and collected tickets. I think I may have even won something, but the night was a blur for me. Besides the joy of knowing my dad was alive—*alive*—it was also beginning to dawn on me that now I would never get a chance to put on a leather helmet and goggles and soar above the city with my dad. *That* dream had ended.

Except (just like with Peter), God wanted something else to happen.

One year after my dad crashed his plane, he had rebuilt it. He finished the fifty hours, and I had the chance to fly with him.

I climbed into the front cockpit—in a bi-plane, the pilot always sits in back—and I put on my goggles and leather helmet, just as I always dreamed I would. My dad climbed in. From the micro-tiny front cockpit, I could observe everything—I saw Dad's legs stretched forward next to mine. I saw the joystick moving. "Don't touch that!" Dad said earlier on his walkie-talkie. I knew better, but I smiled any-way—this was really happening!

As we rumbled down the runway, I could watch Dad actually fly-ing because I could see him using the joystick and navigating with his feet. The wheels separated from the ground, and our crazy angle was leveling off as the world below rushed backward. Stardust Too was taking us straight into the blue sky.

My thoughts were rushing, too. I thought this would never hap-pen—that day in March, I was not only sure I would never fly with my dad, but I was sure I would never see him again. I was like Peter, left with nothing but empty nets filled with crushed dreams. After all, the Lord was dead, wasn't He?

In the days after Stardust Too's crash, it was kind of like that for us, too—while everybody was glad my dad had made it, it was uni-versally believed that his bi-plane dream was dead. The "I told you so's" were flying. It was like everyone had given up on Dad's dream. Maybe the scoffers were right, after all?

My dad knew better. He shrugged off the scolders and naysayers and went about his business. And now we were flying.

Many years later, after my dad had passed away, my mom made sure I got his old logbook. I opened it immediately and flipped back to the year when all Dad's dreams came true. I scrolled down through his meticulously kept entries, and there it was:

First passenger, Starduster Too, my son Eric.

I stared at the words in my dad's neat handwriting, and I couldn't help but think again of Peter and his empty nets. How could he know that the Lord would restore everything? How could he know the Lord would take him to places he never thought he would go?

God didn't mean for crashes to define us. We are all built to fly.

FLIGHT PLANS

Let your mind go free: How could you soar in life if you really let it happen?

What's stopping you?

How do you recover after a crash—loss of a person, a job, financial stability, reputation?

What good has happened—even after a crash?

Where are you right now?

- Dreaming, planning?
- Starting the process of building?
- Taking off – starting to fly?
- Picking up the dreams after a crash?
- Which one do you most relate to today?

PART II:
STEER CLEAR OF THE ROCKS

....

Fair warning: Many are brought down by facts they didn't pay attention to until it was too late

BEACHED

I f you have a blank spot on your bucket list, consider visiting one of the world's most spectacular places, Chatterbox Falls, British Columbia. The only way to get there is through a tricky patch of waterway called the Jervis Inlet, but it's a challenge worth taking. Chatterbox Falls has been ranked by National Geographic Magazine as one of the top ten places to visit in the world.

Getting there is both beautiful and dangerous—just like certain things in life. They look so good, so appealing, that we lose all perspective on whether they are good for us or not. We don't look for the traps. And when we finally see them, it can be too late.

That's what happened to the owner of a handsome yacht called The Golden Cell.

I was close enough to see this disaster unfold. That weekend, I was with some three hundred teenagers and kids at a Young Life event at the Malibu Club, which is located one hundred miles north of Vancouver, British Columbia. This camp was located on that aforementioned tricky patch of waterway—the Jervis Inlet.

How Young Life happened to land in this Canadian paradise called the Malibu Club is worth a little side story. In the early 1950s, a wealthy guy named Hamilton heard the siren's call of this fantastic place, and he decided to build a resort there. He called it the Malibu

Club. He probably picked the name because he was from California, and he was stuck on visions of navy-blue skies and endless sunshine. Clearly, he didn't know the Pacific Northwest or Canadian weather systems. It didn't take long for the rain, fog, and grey clouds to throw a wet blanket over his plans for a magical getaway of golfing, sunbathing, and dancing under the stars.

He was so disillusioned that one day, he up and left—literally. He even left dirty dishes on the table. "I'm out, I'm done," he told friends. Then he put Malibu Club on the market for $1,000,000.

This is where we never underestimate God's ability to change the impossible. It just so happened that the founder of Young Life, Jim Rayburn, took a trip to the Malibu Club, and all he could think was, "Oh, my gosh. This has kids written all over it!" He saw waterskiing, kayaking, hiking, towering mountains, waterways, a setting so spectacular only God could have thought of it. But a million dollars? Out of reach.

Yes, but not to Jim. He had an idea.

Jim tracked down Hamilton and persuaded him to visit a Young Life Camp in Colorado. Hamilton was so impressed with what he saw and so in awe of Young Life's work and mission—to introduce young people to Christ in some of the world's most inspiring, resort-like, adventurous settings—that he decided to help. He sold us Malibu for $300,000—and donated the first $100,000!

And that's how we came to have a front-row seat overlooking the Jervis Inlet, ten miles from Chatterbox Falls, when the yacht called The Golden Cell tried—and failed—to make it to paradise.

Golden Cell yacht

Jervis Inlet, Golden Cell yacht

❊ ❊ ❊

The problem is that the Jervis Inlet is governed by ocean tides, so the yachts must be careful when timing their passage. (I know this myself—I've nosed a 37-foot boat through the inlet, and it made *me* nervous.) The Golden Cell was 220 feet long, with a belly that extended way beneath the surface. The problem, hidden just underneath this apparently fathomless waterway, was a jagged mountain range of rocks, just waiting to impale the unwary boater. No, you go through the Jervis Inlet at high tide, or not at all.

This is where our unlucky yacht owner comes in. Actually, his problem wasn't luck—his problem was arrogance. He figured he could get away with anything he wanted to. He told the captain he had a specific goal for the trip: "I want to wake up tomorrow morning at Chatterbox Falls."

When he made this demand, it was 11 o'clock at night, and the yacht had just entered the Jervis Inlet. Chatterbox Falls was still at least an hour away. "Slack tide," which means exactly what it says, was approaching, and that meant the tide was going out. Given the circumstances, the skipper had some wise advice for the wealthy landlubber: "This is not a good time to go further tonight. Trust me. We can anchor out here and cast off in the morning at 7:00 a.m. You can have your coffee as we're heading up to Chatterbox Falls."

"No!" the yacht owner groused, "I want to *wake up* at Chatterbox Falls!" The captain tried to reason with him. The boat was massive— a helicopter and two ski boats were perched on top—and this was no time to fool around in a shallow inlet. The captain tried again. "Sir, it's 11 o'clock at night, we're approaching low tide, it's dangerous to move ahead!"

The yacht owner wouldn't budge. He was determined to wake up the next morning nowhere else but at Chatterbox Falls. After going back and forth to the point of exhaustion, the captain gave in.

After all, it wasn't *his* yacht!

The result was that the next morning, the most astonishing sight wasn't at Chatterbox Falls; it was the spectacle we saw from Malibu's Flag Point.

About five hundred yards away from our cabin, the once handsome Golden Cell was splayed like a beached whale on a pile of rocks. A crowd was gathering. By then, the foolish yacht owner had slunk away from the wreck, probably to call his insurance carrier. The humiliated captain was ferried over to us at the Malibu Club. As you can expect, he didn't talk much.

Like all personal disasters, the after-effects radiated way beyond the first bad decision. A professional diver, a local guy named Mike, wrote about it in a blog, saying it was a life-changing, even legendary, event to rescue The Golden Cell. Working with him was a salvage expert, a tugboat team, and eventually, the Coast Guard, which had some uncomfortable questions for the skipper *and* the owner. In the end, The Golden Cell ("The biggest yacht I'd ever laid eyes on," blogged Mike) was no more. It was claimed as salvage.

Years later, I can still see that elegant vessel grounded on the shoals like a bloated, ugly duckling. What a waste! The yacht owner was so arrogant he didn't want to see what was ahead. But the captain was at fault, too. He also was not willing to face the fact that there were rocks beneath the surface that he could not see but were dangerous. He was the one who decided to inch through Jervis Inlet in the middle of the night, and maybe because of all the radar and sonar equipment on board, he thought he could get away with it. A lot of good it did him. All he saw was a mini lighthouse and smooth water ahead. He couldn't see the rocks. *But he had all the warnings to know they were there.*

Isn't it just like life? The rocks that bring us down are all under the surface. Is it a marriage in trouble or a growing affection for alcohol or pornography? Or maybe it's just a little innocent flirting at a party that turns into a nagging itch for something more? Or what about that gray area on the office expense account? It sits there, widening a little every year because the boss probably won't notice? I believe that if you look hard enough, everybody can look at their life and identify the rocks underneath.

Of course, Satan is the ultimate deceiver, who makes sure to hide those rocks as best he can. But think about it: If Satan wanted to take *you* out, how would he do it? I have seen staff that I know—really good people—taken out for things like DUIs, fraud, making fake invoices, taking money in the form of petty cash, as well as having an affair or dangerously engaging with pornography. "The thief comes to steal, kill, and destroy." (John 10:10) And he does it with hidden rocks beneath the surface. You cannot impact people if you are taken out. Live your life the best you can with your eyes wide open!

And one more thing... remember Eph. 4:27: "Don't give the devil a foothold!" My last note to all of you is this – Satan can get a grip on "little things" that at the time seem small. I remember having my son with me while we watched a "climbing wall" get constructed. The man putting it together was putting on all the tiny rocks... some yellow, some green, some blue, and some red. I remember asking him, wow, those yellow ones look so small. He said, oh, these climbers can grip them and navigate all the way up to the top! Rocks are beneath the surface for sure, and some can get attached to us. What little rocks might the evil one use to get a better grip on your life?

FLIGHT PLANS

Be honest with yourself: What hidden rocks are you avoiding in life?

Is there a person you know who is about to make a big mistake in *their* life? Can you do anything to help them hear the warning bell?

Can you think back to a time when you crashed on the rocks? What did you learn from that? Can you use that experience to help someone else?

THE BIG HOUSE

Why do we have to be reminded again and again of that old saying, "Things are not always as they seem"? I learned that valuable lesson while I was still in high school.

At the time, I had a good friend, Peder, whose dad lived on a farm. The farm was pretty modest, but there was an unusual thing about the property: His dad built a little one-story country house that he lived in, but off on another side of the farm was a really interesting 1920s Victorian mansion with a cupola and wraparound porch, and lots of spooky-looking windows, just the kinds of things that teenage boys are crazy to explore. Although we had never been inside, in the estimation of all of us guys, it was a *very* cool house.

Just as cool as the Big House (that's what we called it) was Peder's dad. He was a very unique guy. He had been a shop teacher for his whole career, but then he really got into farming, and he started planting bean fields. We were always going out to help him pick beans, which was okay except in the blazing summer heat.

What we liked even more was helping Peter's dad with his car restorations.

Cars were his big passion. I guess it stemmed from his work as a shop teacher. All things mechanical and anything having to do with welding and restoring cars interested Peder's dad.

One day, Peder said, "Hey, guys, we've got to get a new radiator for dad's 1925 International truck. We can find one at the Big House."

Now, this was an adventure! For the first time, we were actually going *inside* the Big House. I imagined exploring gloomy hallways and climbing rickety stairs to the cobwebby attic, maybe waving off bats swooping down from the rafters.

As we trudged toward the Big House, I really let my imagination take off—maybe we'd even find treasures lurking in the corners or peeking out from the floorboards, like long-lost gold coins!

As we came to the front door, we could hardly keep from running up the steps. Okay, what treasures were waiting for us inside the Big House? Peder unlocked the door and led us in.

Dumbfounded, we just stood there. No treasures and no gold coins. Not even a bat swinging from the ceiling.

No, the entire living room was packed with *radiators.* In the first bedroom to the right of the kitchen, all we could see was a jumbled pile of small engines. The upstairs bedroom had been taken over by fenders—hundreds of fenders.

We couldn't believe it. The Big House of our dreams, and all the magic we imagined behind that front door—it was really just a supply house of junked cars!

"How did this happen?" I just had to ask Peder, although I didn't want to tell him what I really thought—that this cool house was nothing but a dirty old junkyard behind a closed door.

Peder looked pretty embarrassed. "Look," he said and went over to the door and tried to close it. It wouldn't shut. He went around to the back of the house, and I went around to the back of the house with him. We stood in the little patch of land and looked up at the house, and I couldn't believe what I saw.

From the back, the house was literally leaning into the ground at an angle. It looked like an ocean liner that was sinking on its side into the sea.

"Wow," I said and then repeated myself. "How did this happen?"

"Well," Peder said, "my dad rented this house ten years ago to a family. They wanted to put in a basement. Here's what happened."

He led me down some broken old steps to the basement. Sure enough, the renters had dug and dug, expecting to be digging out a fine basement.

What they didn't know, they were literally digging the foundation out from under the house. They were just carving it away. When they finally moved out, the doors and windows weren't shutting, and the floors were sloping. The walls were cracking and bulging.

The house was toast.

When I think of the Big House now, it reminds me that in life, what's on the outside may bear no relationship to what's inside. Be careful. Eventually, it's the foundation that always tells the truth.

In fact, disastrous foundations are talked about in the Bible. One of the most vivid is the reporting, by Christ Himself, in Luke 13:1, of the collapse of the tower of Siloam that killed eighteen people. This stunning disaster was clearly the talk of the day—Christ even mentions the number of people killed, which means the news had to be still fresh in everybody's minds. Then, of course, there is the famous lesson from Scripture in Matthew 7:24, when Christ warns of the house with the disastrous foundation: *"And everyone who hears these words of mine and does not do them will be like a foolish man who built his house on the sand ... and the rain fell, and the floods came, and the winds blew and beat against that house, and it fell, and great was the fall of it."*

Whether our downfall comes from unseen rocks or from crumbling foundations, there are usually no warnings until it's too late. But that doesn't mean we're off the hook. What are the key foundational pieces that hold your "house" and/or your life together? The goal of having a healthy and strong foundation is that it keeps the house up! The tower of Siloam fell probably due to two things: (1) Secret sin and (2) repentance. What would be your foundation's key aspects? Is it a quiet time, date nights, church on Sunday, working out, time with your kids, family vacations, or knowing God's word? Whatever these key moments are—when you don't allow yourself time, then you are slowly digging out your foundation.

We all need fair warnings now and then. *Pay attention.*

Here's another story about things not being what they seem:

RUSSIAN CHOCOLATE

One of my covenant brothers went to Russia on a mission trip when he was just out of high school. On his way back, he and a buddy were forced to spend all night in some anonymous and deserted airport because of an airline scheduling glitch.

They had spent a month traveling, and they expected to be home by now, which is why they had run out of money. They were exhausted and seriously hungry.

Now, this airport was the opposite of a bustling international hub; there was no one there. It was the middle of the night, and the only other person they saw was a glum-looking maintenance guy sweeping the same empty concourse over and over again.

About the time their hunger headaches started, one of the guys noticed a display in one of the kiosks. It was a candy display. Behind the glass, they could see the swelling mounds of chocolate wrapped in gold foil—rows and rows of dark and succulent Russian chocolate.

Temptation and hunger were hard at work on these guys. My buddy and his friend scanned the airport aisles. Even the maintenance guy had shuffled away. The airport was as empty as their stomachs, and they had another eight hours to go.

My friend's buddy said, "You know, it would be amazing if we could ever so slightly get into that display. I'm so hungry, and it looks so good!"

They looked some more at those mounds of gold-wrapped Russian chocolate, and it inspired them to think along a certain line. One of them reasoned this way: "It's not right that no stores are open to get some food. If we can get at that chocolate, we'll repay the shop people later."

After they had reasoned in their minds, it was a short hop to devising an actual break-in. One of them was going to stand at a strategic corner of the airport so he could keep a lookout up and down the concourse to make sure nobody was coming by. Meanwhile, the other guy was going to work on the display by trying to bend the glass enough to get at the lock. After twenty minutes, they would reverse places.

Their scheme worked. Eventually, the display front separated about an inch, which was just enough to slide the glass and reach in and grab the mouth-watering chocolate in the gold wrappers.

Next, they headed for a restroom to divide up the loot, and they also agreed to stay apart for the next four hours in case anyone got suspicious.

"See you at the gate," my friend said to his buddy.

As soon as he was alone, my friend opened up his gold-foiled chocolate with trembling fingers. He was so hungry. If they were exhausted before, that was nothing compared to the exhaustion of pulling off the chocolate caper!

But now the payoff came. My friend bit down on the chocolate with the enthusiasm of a kid biting into his own birthday cake.

A second later, he was gagging. The chocolate had turned to dust. It was in that alluring display case for who knows how long? A decade or more! The pretty gold foil was like smooth water over rocks or a house with no foundation. It was nothing but a trap for the bad stuff hidden inside.

James 1:15 says: *"After desire has conceived, it gives birth to sin; and sin, when it is full-grown, gives birth to death."* This is talking about foiled chocolate, smooth water, or the desire to dig out a basement.

Little decisions have a way of growing and taking on a life of their own. And sometimes, when they are decisions that have grown to something larger, they can take us out and disqualify us from what and who we really want to be.

Isn't this the way some things are in this world that probably aren't the best for us? They lure us in; with gold embossed foil, they look so good. We often, or should I say, I often am, looking at different things in life and am swept up by the foil. It could be a job, a home, a car, or a boat. It could be a relationship, a trip, or a multitude of things on social media. I find I get the "If onlys!" If only I had this or that—it's a lure.

FLIGHT PLANS

- What lures have you followed in life, only to find they are nothing but tinsel and dust?
- The bible says that sin will "zap" you like the noon day sun. "He will bring forth your righteousness as a light, and your justice as the noonday sun." Ps. 37:6. So, where has your energy been taken away from choices you have made?
- And, what does this quote mean to you: **"Sin will take you farther than you want to go, keep you longer than you want to stay, and cost you more than you want to pay. –"** R Zaccharias

ONE MORE THING

There is one "kid-sitting" job I will never forget. I've never forgotten this story because I was directly involved and because I saw how it turned out. Let's just say there are some kinds of looming disasters that don't cause shipwrecks or foundation collapses; some disasters are lying in wait to shatter the soul. Why should we be surprised when we know "the whole world is in control of the Evil One." (John 5:19)

I was about twenty-five years old when I learned this lesson about the absolute need to confess all sins—*especially* those we would rather keep covered, deep inside us. At a time and place I never expected, I learned the wisdom of James 5:16: *"Confess your faults one to another, and pray one for another, that you may be healed."*

The story begins on a very relaxed weekend around the time of spring break. A major part of my job as a Youth leader was to be ready to be a guide and mentor to any kid who needed it, no matter what the circumstances. In this case, the parents of a high school sophomore asked if I would stay with their son while they began the family's spring vacation. As soon as school let out, about a week later, my job was to get their son on a plane so he could join them.

Jared was a great kid, so I was looking forward to being his "sitter" for a week. He was easy to be with—he was immersed in sports and was always on the go. That meant all I really had to do was come up with dinners for a ravenous kid and be ready in the evening for the challenging questions that teens love to throw at you—questions about life, sports, girls, his future, and everything he was learning from the Lord.

Jared had his head on straight. He was an all-around super young man from a good family, the kind of teenager that's easy to interact with. I didn't see an uptight bone in his body. He called me Sco (like everybody did), and I felt I knew him well enough to get on his back a little if he was slacking off chores. If I said something like, "Hey, Jared, get off the couch and help me feed the dishwasher!" he'd grin and jump right up. He was *that* kind of kid. So, if I ever was wary of spending an entire week with a teenager I didn't know that well (after all, I was only in my mid-twenties), that hesitancy vanished by the end of the first day. I was sorry to see the week come to an end.

As we drove to the airport, our conversations continued. It got even more intense, probably because our time together was winding down. Jared was still pounding me with questions—good questions. I guess you could say they all were about living a moral life in this crazy world. I was challenging him back, too, asking him about his goals for the summer, and deeper questions—how did he intend to follow the Lord, especially as he got older and was more involved with worldly jobs and meeting kids he didn't know? "What do you feel that God wants you to do in your life?" I asked, and later, I challenged him with this: "Is there anything that God's whispering to you that you're not doing yet?"

Our communication was fast and easy, kind of like a good tennis match. A few times, between the banter and friendly back-and-forths,

Jared fell silent and stared out the window. I respected that. Kids need space to think and consider things.

Then, suddenly, we were at PDX, Portland International Airport. We got the car parked, hoisted Jared's gear on our shoulders, and headed for the gate. (This was in the easy days before security lines and TSA guards.) As we strolled to the gate, I reflected on the important week we had. I felt Jared had grown a lot in his understanding of God, and I felt I had done my part, too, by showing him ways to be a young man of integrity in this uncertain world. And I can't deny that I was looking forward to heading home and catching up on my own life, too.

Finally, it was time for the awkward airport goodbye. "So long, Jared, have a good trip, and say hi to your folks," I said. Jared thanked me for my hospitality, and we shook hands. For a moment, it seemed like he might have something else to ask me, so I prodded him a little, "Everything okay?" "Oh yeah, everything's good," Jared said. Then he shot one last grin at me and turned to walk up the boarding ramp.

Mission accomplished! I felt good about everything, and just to be sure—I didn't tell Jared—but I was going to hang around the airport until his plane took off, just so I knew he was safely on his way. I started sauntering down the concourse, relieved and happy the week had gone so well, and maybe a little glad I was free of the responsibilities at last.

What I remembered next, I remember as though it were happening all over again. Suddenly, I hear a shout behind me. By that time, I'm two gates past where I left Jared off. I realize that shout was my name.

"Sco! Sco!"

"I turn and see Jared running down the concourse toward me at a full clip. As he reaches me, he gasps, **"There's one more thing!"**

I said, "Yeah? What's the one more thing? How can I help?"

Where was the easy-going kid I had said goodbye to just three minutes before? He had vanished. This young man's face was twisted up with pain and embarrassment. He blurted out his next words fast, like he couldn't wait to get rid of them.

"When you get back to my house, I want you to go downstairs to my bedroom and open the closet. There are three boxes on the top shelf. The box on the bottom—pull that out and open it up."

"Sure, Jared …"

"I mean it, Sco, open it up and pull everything out of it!" The kid was in real pain. I could tell it cost him a lot to tell me this. I could see the next part was especially hard: "There's a fake bottom in the box. Pull that out, too. Everything you see—would you throw it all away?"

Even as the last words came out of his mouth, I watched his face start to relax. He had done something hard, and he was glad he had done it.

"Jared, I would be happy to do this for you," I said the words slowly because I wanted to impress on his mind that his request—his plea, really—was safe with me. I would do exactly what he asked. I wanted to reassure him because I could see it cost him a lot to open up to me. Without saying a word, he gave me a hug and, clearly with a lighter step, bounced back toward his gate.

When I got to his house, I did what he asked. I couldn't help but see what was in the fake bottom of the box because everything was tossed in there openly, as if Jared believed his secret would be safe forever.

Let's just say Jared had the kind of secrets that make us all go, "Wow, I never would have guessed." No wonder it was so hard for him to tell me.

At the bottom of the box was a stash of marijuana and a collection of pornography magazines. I got a garbage bag and wrapped everything so securely that no one would bother to check what was inside. As soon as I left his house, I discarded the mess in a public trash bin.

We all create fake bottoms in our box—the box that's our *life*. We want people to see just the outside of the box—or the top half of it—which is our best side, our most admirable qualities, the parts that make people go, "What a great person!" But we all have things stuffed away. I have learned this over and over. We all cover up. We even create plans to hide what we don't want others to see.

The Lord was working on Jared's heart, and he was willing to respond to the Lord by confessing his sins to a fellow believer. It's as if the Lord is saying, *"Jared, you know there's one more thing. Just get rid of it."*

Driving home after I had thrown Jared's "hidden life" in the trash, I felt so happy for that kid! Aloud, I said, "When you come home from your trip, Jared, it's gonna be gone, all gone from your life!" Even before that, I knew when he got on that plane, his backpack was lighter.

At a young age, Jared was blessed to learn the truth about the hidden rocks in his life. *We all have them.* These rocks are the unconfessed sins that can throw us off course, like a beautiful yacht that's shipwrecked on a beach, or they can crush us in a disaster that can last a lifetime, like a failed marriage, or alcoholism, or even prison. Whether the rocks are big or small, we can be stopped cold from living the life God intends us to live.

And sometimes unconfessed sins just wear us away, year after year, like the house Peder's dad built. These hidden sins are buried so deep that we don't even realize that our foundation—our integrity as a person—is being eroded year after year by sins that have drawn us away from God. These are the sins that isolate us, little by little, from the people we love. Our foundation has become just a shell.

Jared was blessed. He recognized the *"one more thing"* that could mess up his life forever. He did something about it.

Have you?

FLIGHT PLANS

What's your "One more thing?"

ACTION PLAN: Find a quiet place where you have the time and serenity to review your life. If you can spare a weekend, visit a retreat house, or take a road trip to an inspiring location where you can empty your mind of the daily grind, which will give you the freedom to reflect.

Establish the foundation of your time away by inviting the Lord to be there with you:

"Lord, help me acknowledge my unconfessed sins and hidden life. I know you want the best for me and my family, and these sins are holding me back from being the person you called me to be.

With your help, Lord, I confess these sins to you ...

Now, Lord, guide me to the trustworthy person on earth who will hear my sins confidentially, a person who will support and encourage me to create a new life of integrity."

ASK YOURSELF:

- Who would you feel comfortable confessing to?
- How has your unconfessed, hidden life affected your family?
- Has hidden life made you less "present" to your family, friends, and colleagues than before?
- Have you become distant or short-tempered because of a hidden life?
- In what ways have you seen having a hidden life creating financial hardships?
- Can you see where a hidden life could create larger issues?
- How would your life be more free, more unburdened if you put the hidden life behind you?

THE YELLOW TARP

I t was 1982, a rainy, windy, and cold November night in Salem, Oregon, and our high school football team was in the playoffs for the state championship. I was one of the kids in the stands, watching the South Salem Saxons fight (literally) to the finish. In fact, the score was still 0-0 at the end of regulation play. A win was all in the hands—or rather, the foot—of our kicker, Ed Johnson. He was our last chance to get on the board. Ed made a great decision to kick a little to the side of the goalposts to take advantage of the stiff wind (gusts were twenty to thirty mph that night), and it worked! The ball sailed straight between the posts like it was on a zipline. Beautiful! Game over. We win. The next round of the playoffs—bring it on!

Even in the wind and icy rain, "giddy" pretty much describes the mood. The whole high school had turned out for this game, plus there was a swarm of alums, all the family members, and probably all the friends the team ever had. This game was a big deal. And at the end of it, everybody had the same idea—pizza!

I had the car that night, and a few of my high school buddies and I decided to celebrate at Pietro's, one of our favorite pizza joints. We ordered sodas and warm, greasy pepperoni pizza—just the thing for a rainy night in Salem. Then our celebration wound down, and it was time to drive my passengers, Peder, Greg, and Steve, back to their homes.

I made a turn on a main street in downtown Salem, and suddenly, in front of us, all we saw was an explosion of red, yellow, and blue lights. As we got closer, we saw the lights were coming from a huge clump of police cars, fire trucks, and ambulances. We couldn't tell what happened, but our first reaction was clear—we wanted to help. As we inched our way to a place to pull over, our curiosity took over.

I barely had the car parked when the guys piled out and raced for the barricade. (There are certain things that high school boys are drawn to, and they often involve things like "keep out" signs and barricades.) It's only when we get some wisdom that we realize barricades are often good because they prevent you from entering accident scenes, hospital rooms, and most situations that involve the opposite sex.

In this case, it must have been the adrenaline of the victory that night, the celebration (don't forget the pizza) that made us unstoppable. Everybody crowded around the scene. Best we could tell, this was a two-car accident.

Then, we saw the crushed and twisted motorcycle near the curb. It was undeniably exciting to stand there in the pool of flashing lights, with chaos and destruction all around us. We were talking a mile a minute.

"It looks like that car was hit by the other car."

"Nahh ... it looks like the motorcycle hit the car first."

"Yeah, you're right. When the motorcycle hit the first car, it spun and rammed into the second car ..."

"... and look at the telephone pole! It isn't broken, but it sure looks bent over from the impact!"

We were so eager to figure out how this happened that we could have been a crew of accident re-enactment specialists. Then, in the middle of our excitement and speculation frenzy, we noticed something that didn't make sense. It wasn't a car, and it wasn't the motorcycle. It was a yellow tarp.

"I wonder what that is?"

As we stared at the yellow tarp, a gust of hard, Oregon wind suddenly blasted over us. I will never forget that wind. It gave us the answer to the yellow tarp.

The yellow tarp flew up and exposed the body of a lone, dead motorcyclist. He was lying there in a way that a body does not naturally lie. His legs were all askew, like a rag doll. A small stream of very bright, red blood flowed from his head. In the bright lights, we could see his crumpled-up face had turned purple-gray. It was a sight I will never forget. None of us would. We were silent.

The police scrambled to get the yellow tarp back in place. But it was too late. I had seen the reality of this situation. Long before anyone in the family knew that their beloved father, son, or husband was dead, *I* knew he was dead. A bunch of strangers knew he was dead. I struggled to process what I was seeing.

Here was a person who had life running at full force, not just on the street that night, but 24/7. He had a job, a list of future plans, people he loved, and someone who was expecting him to come home that night. A warm bed was waiting for him. I saw the truth in one sickening moment; this was a human being, like me, but this human being was not coming home.

I won't kid you—I liked it better when the yellow tarp was in place. It hid the truth. While the yellow tarp was in place, we could speculate in our innocence about the "cool wreck" and debate the factors that made it happen. We couldn't do that now. Our excitement (not to mention our innocence) was as crushed as the poor guy under the yellow tarp.

Later, we realized all our thoughts had been circling around the same thing: the life of this stranger was snatched away from him just about the moment Ed Johnson was aiming the winning kick. Or maybe it was at the moment we were ordering our large, $5.99 warm and greasy pepperoni pizza.

None of us were thinking those thoughts while the yellow tarp was still covering up everything underneath. Later, I realized something about life that is not necessarily admirable or good, but it exists: *The yellow tarp is universal.* It covers up, plain and simple, the ugly things we don't want to know about. The yellow tarp hides the things that would shock us. The yellow tarp makes it better for everyone when we don't know what's underneath. It just does.

Isn't "covering up" the message of our world? "Wear black, it hides bulges." "Don't tell them now; what they don't know can't hurt them." The examples are endless. "Look young" (even though you're not). "Look like you have money" (even though you don't), and generally cover up every defeat and sadness because they make you look weak and vulnerable!

That scene has never left me. And it's made me think about two friends who covered up their own wounds beneath a yellow tarp.

We were at a national Young Life property during a Leadership Camp. One day, one of the younger leaders rushed out of her cabin, blood gushing from her face. "I went to take a shower and slipped on the bathroom floor," she explained. "I'm so embarrassed!" We got her to a doctor, and she came back to camp sporting three stitches. End of drama.

However, this young woman did not slip on the bathroom floor while taking a shower.

It turned out that Ashley had excused herself from breakfast to go back to the cabin to throw up. Ashley had a serious, full-blown eating disorder.

Many months later, Ashley allowed us to pull back the edges of *her* yellow tarp, and we saw the wounds on her heart. This normal, wholesome-looking young woman thought she was "fat." She was running after a kind of perfection that doesn't exist anywhere but in the air-brushed photos of teen magazines. When she allowed us to pull back the tarp even more, we saw a girl whose father abandoned her when she was two years old and who tried to make up for that loss by being with the wrong guy. Then she got pregnant. She placed her baby in adoption, which was the courageous and right decision but a deeply painful one that added to her list of wounds.

No, on the slick and tidy side of the yellow tarp, things are not always what they seem.

Another time, I was spending a good deal of energy encouraging a kid to join a Young Life trip to the Oregon coast. Matt was a very cool and accomplished kid, and I was sure he'd learn a lot and be an asset to the group. As I was driving him home from an event, I really pressed him hard—but he kept saying no, no, he couldn't come with us. But why?

We pulled up to his house, a stately mansion with a wide manicured lawn, landscape lighting, and a Lincoln Town Car in the curved drive. I admit I kept pressing him hard, but I had to. It's part of my job at Young Life to know what's going on with a kid, especially if he seems in trouble. I wondered if Matt was having a problem with one of the other kids, and if so, it was my job to know.

Suddenly, this young man burst into tears. "Please ... I can't go ... I want to, but I can't!"

Now, I was perplexed. I really had to know because, clearly, something was seriously wrong. "But Matt, why?"

Matt took a big gulp of air and stripped away his yellow tarp. He told me that his family had nothing. The huge stately mansion was a sham. The cupboards inside were bare, and the curtains never opened because they had virtually no inside furniture to show off. His dad was battling bankruptcy. Through sobs, Matt said his parents swore him to secrecy, which is why he couldn't explain that he didn't have the money for the $55 weekend.

I was shocked, dumbfounded. I would have never guessed this, not in a million years. On this kid's life, the yellow tarp had been pulled extra tight.

Yellow tarps—we all have them. A long time after seeing that first yellow tarp, I was speaking at a camp in front of four hundred and twenty-five kids. These kids were the cream of the crop; they had looks, possessions, and great futures.

"Do any of you really have any *real* needs?" I asked. These kids were smart, too, and they thought they knew what I meant, so they smiled and shook their heads, "No." "Listen," I said, "you all say you have everything you need. But I know the truth. No matter how good-looking you think you are, how smart you are, how much money your parents have—the truth is, *everyone has a yellow tarp.*"

After my talk, the kids went to their cabins to discuss my talk with each other and their leaders. After the discussion groups, we had an entertainment program planned for that evening, capped by a festive "all you can eat" round of banana splits.

But that night, only half the kids turned up for the entertainment and banana splits. The other two hundred kids never left their cabins.

Why? They all wanted to pull back and talk about their "yellow tarps." The talk had struck a chord with these teens. Afterward, the leaders said it was the best cabin time they had ever had with their groups.

The reason it resonated, of course, is because *everyone* has a yellow tarp! Often, the most therapeutic thing in the world is to be able to pull it back and talk about what's underneath.

It turns out yellow tarps are as old as history. In fact, there's a great "yellow tarp" moment in Scripture, in John: 4:1-42, when we meet the woman at the well. Jesus asks her for a cup of water, and then He draws her into a conversation. We know now that Christ initiated the conversation because He wanted to help the woman draw back her yellow tarp. (Pretty much like the conversations the kids had in their cabins.)

Jesus was able to draw out from the woman that she has been keeping a big and shameful secret—that she had five husbands, and her current "husband" didn't really qualify. With that revelation came healing.

Christ wants us to know the same healing is possible *today.* He was teaching us that we are designed to share our lives and to open up with others. And you know what? We end up being closer to the people who are there with us as we pull back our own yellow tarp.

FLIGHT PLANS
What's Under Your Yellow Tarp?

ACTION PLAN: Pulling back the tarp is never easy. So, pick a quiet place where you can give yourself the time to reflect and be still. Surround yourself in a spirit of mercy and gentleness. Remember, the yellow tarp is not about unconfessed sin—that *"one more thing"*—no, it's about the realities in your life that are too painful, sad, or ugly to talk about, and you think you must keep them hidden.

ASK YOURSELF:

- What IS under your tarp? Can you identify it?
- Name a person you trust enough to share this with. (Remember, they have tarps, too.)
- What is one action you could take to pull back the tarp from your life so you can heal?
- Imagine one thing about your life that would be better if you could face what was under the yellow tarp.
- Reach out to one person who is hurting and encourage them to share their tarp with you.

YODA AND THE HOBO

When a teenage boy walks into a pancake house, it's usually to fill a craving for a double order of pigs in a blanket and a side of pancakes. You aren't usually expecting one of those "I have to talk to you" conversations.

When Pete walked into the Original Pancake House a few days after Halloween, all seemed well. I was there having breakfast with Jack, another Young Life leader.

"Hey Pete, what's going on?" We both knew Pete, one of the most well-liked kids in that sophomore year. He was a good athlete and one of the more popular guys at school. This was about four days after Halloween, and we knew all the kids had been amped up with parties. A big football game was coming up, too. Jack and I were interested in catching up with Pete.

Pretty quickly, we saw that Pete wasn't there to talk about football. His hair was still wet like he had just leaped out of the shower. His letterman's jacket was sitting lopsided on one shoulder like he had literally thrown it on.

"I have to talk to you," Pete said.

"Sure thing, Pete, what you got?"

This kid, usually happy and down-to-earth, couldn't look us in the eye. Now, we were concerned, but we knew we had to give him space to unpack his story.

"On Halloween," he said slowly, "I had my mom's car, and my buddies and I were driving around, and, well, we came up with this idea. The idea was, "let's steal a kid's candy.""

When a young person tells you something shocking, it's important to stay quiet. Let the whole story come out. Pete still couldn't look at us, but at least he was talking.

Pete and his buddies were dressed for Halloween—Pete was wearing a Yoda "Star Wars" mask—but this year, they needed something more exciting than going door to door asking for candy. That seemed dumb. "Trick or Treat" is for little kids. (Let them do the boring stuff, ringing doorbells, asking for candy! It's more fun to just get candy *without* doing the dumb stuff!) That was their thinking, anyway. Pete forced the story out, with every painful detail, until we could almost see it unfold right before our eyes.

They started cruising the streets, looking for a good mark. The longer it took, the better the idea became. Then, "all of a sudden, right in front of us, was this kid."

He was a skinny little kid who looked to be ten or eleven years old. He was dressed like a hobo. He was all by himself, not going up to doors anymore, just trudging along the sidewalk like he was heading for home.

"We couldn't believe it," Pete said, "especially cuz he was lugging the biggest pillowcase of candy we had ever seen."

In the space it took to say, "Let's go!" the five teenagers turned into full-fledged bandits. Pete told his fellow conspirators, "You guys drive ahead. I'll grab the candy and meet you in the grade school parking lot."

Behind his mask, Yoda was on a high. This was going to be great! He hit the sidewalk about a half block ahead of the Hobo. When they met in the center of the sidewalk, Yoda was ready. In one swipe, he snatched the pillowcase—cool!—swung around and took off.

But Yoda had underestimated his mark. Behind him, he heard the Hobo shriek in anger and surprise. Next thing he knew, the Hobo had tackled him in one flying leap.

This caper was not going as planned. The Hobo was stronger than Yoda thought—rage had made him strong. Finally (this wasn't a game anymore), Yoda hauled back and slugged the Hobo. The kid gave a grunt of pain and collapsed on the sidewalk.

The getaway car pulled up, and Yoda took one last glance at the Hobo. The kid looked pathetic. He was still struggling to stand up. His costume was supposed to be funny—he was dressed like an old-fashioned, train-hopping hobo, wearing a striped shirt and suspenders, with short black pants and an old-style cap. He had black marker on his face for a make-believe beard. He was dressed up to have fun. Now, he was gasping for air and tottering as he tried to stand up. Pete could see his striped shirt was torn at the elbow, and something dark was trickling from a bare knee.

Can't think about that now. Pete's buddies pulled up, he threw the pillowcase of candy in the car, and they peeled off into the night. Four blocks away, they swung into the elementary school parking lot. This is what they wanted all night long—to enjoy their haul.

As he told us this part, Pete's eyes were still glued to the table. "We thought it would be fun," he said slowly, "but all of a sudden, we got pretty bummed out. One of the kids in the back says, 'No thanks, I don't want any.' Another kid said he didn't want any, either. In the end, nobody wanted any candy. Not even me."

Jack and I stayed quiet because we sensed Pete needed to say something else. Finally, for the first time since he came up to our table, he looked at us. He had tears in his eyes. "I got to get my life back," he whispered. "I feel awful."

At first, I didn't know what to say. I wasn't just shocked; I was sad. This kid—this nice kid—had done something that was not just criminal but sinful. Worse, he had hurt somebody who was smaller and weaker than himself. In the silence, I began to pray in my spirit, *"Lord, show me how to respond to this young man."*

Almost instantly, the Lord answered my prayer. "Pete," I said, "what you did is serious, but we know the Lord is with us in times of trouble. You did the right thing to come here. So, let's start by praying right now, here at the table."

As we prayed, the Lord cleared the way, and I knew what I should say next. It was the powerful message in James 5:15-16: *"The prayer of the faithful shall save the sick, and the Lord shall raise him up; and if he has committed sins, they shall be forgiven him. Confess your faults one to another, and pray one for another, that you may be healed."*

As I prayed the words over Pete's confession, his body language changed. He went from suffering to surrender. Then he whispered, "I got to find him. I got to say I'm sorry!"

Of course, Jack and I supported that, but inside my heart, I knew that wasn't realistic. They had been cruising around so much they didn't even know the Hobo's neighborhood. And to recognize the Hobo without his costume? Yet, faith told me I had to not only support Pete's desire to find him, but I had to encourage it because it was the right thing to do.

"Listen, Pete," I said, "if the Lord wants you to find this kid, you'll find him. If He wants you to have the opportunity to make restitution, it will happen. Let's pray for that."

After we prayed, the Lord put on my heart something else Pete needed to hear: "If the Lord doesn't provide the opportunity to say you're sorry to the person you wronged, you need to know that you did something important today. You confessed your sin. God assures us in Scripture that when we do wrong, He provides the path to forgiveness, just as it says in James 5: "*by confessing to each other.*"

As we got up from the table, we all realized that something powerful had happened. Pete's face had that shiny, streaky look left by recent tears, but he also looked relieved, even healed. And *thankful.* In fact, that's what he said: "Thanks for listening to me. I didn't know what to do, except I knew I had to tell you."

I was still thinking about Pete when, three or four days later, I took a father-son group to a little cookout weekend at Wi-Ne-Ma, a Christian camp on the Oregon coast. We were meeting another group of young people with their dads. I remember we burned the taco lunch (culinary arts isn't exactly a dad-thing), but we were having so much fun that it didn't matter. At the end of lunch, I found a quiet place for everybody to gather around for a little teaching moment. After we dads had been sufficiently mocked for our cooking abilities, I asked, "So, how you guys doing? What's on your mind these days?"

For some reason, I added, "How was your Halloween?"

Immediately, I sensed tension. The guys in the new group just looked at each other. Then, one of them said to one of his buddies, "C'mon. Tell him what happened."

The kid looked down and mumbled, "I'm so tired of telling this."

"Whoa, what's going on?" I said, and then everybody jumped in to push the kid to tell his story. "Okay, one more time," he said with a big sigh.

"I went trick or treating in a hobo costume, and I guess people feel sorry for hobos cuz I got a lot of candy that night. More candy than my friends did. They wanted to keep going, but I had enough candy, and I wanted to go home. So, I was walking home alone, and out of nowhere, a guy dressed as Yoda grabbed my pillowcase with the candy. I chased him down and tackled him. He wasn't all that strong, and I thought I was gonna get my candy back, but then he hauled off and hit me. I was pretty out of it then, but I think a car pulled up, and Yoda got in, and they took off."

Everybody was quiet. (Me, maybe most of all. Halfway through his story, I had started to pray). "Man, my parents were so ticked off," the Hobo said. "They couldn't believe it—they kept saying, 'Who would do that?' My mom cried. It was supposed to be a fun night. That's the last time I go out for Halloween!" Everybody was so quiet that a feather dropping from the sky would have been louder.

"Let me ask you a question," I said. "If I told you that you could meet Yoda, would you want to?"

"Well, my *parents* would want to," the kid said, and everybody kind of laughed. Then he said, "Yeah, I would like to meet Yoda if I could."

"Well, Yoda wants to meet you, too," I said.

That night, I called Pete. "Tomorrow," I said, "I'm picking you up after school, and we're going to the junior high to meet Hobo. Between now and then, you have to figure out a way to get as much candy as possible into a pillowcase, and when you hand it over to Hobo, you're gonna tell him that the guy who took his candy and knocked him down is not the person you want to be. You're gonna tell him, 'I let peer pressure get to me, and I feel horrible. I am so sorry. Here's your candy, and I'll never forget this as long as I live.'"

Pete couldn't believe he had been given this opportunity. The next day, we pulled up to the junior high school. I stayed in my car as Pete got out with his loaded pillowcase and walked over to the spot where Hobo said he'd be waiting. The two met. What they said, I don't know, but it was *good*. Pete was willing to do something very hard, and that's how he found peace again. When he confessed his sin, God showed His approval by providing exactly the right miracle—bringing him together with the stranger he had wronged. Who could have imagined that? Out of all the kids who lived between central Oregon and the Pacific coast, God arranged that Yoda and the Hobo could meet each other, so *each of them* could be healed!

I don't understand everything about confession and forgiveness— I'm working on it like everybody else—but what I do know is that when we confess to one another, God can either steer us away from the rocks or heal us after we collide with them. As John 1:9 promises: *"If we confess our sins, He is faithful and just, to forgive us our sins and to cleanse us from all unrighteousness."* And to make us whole! The best part about this whole moment—everyone was restored and "healed" from the different aspects of pain that they incurred. The pain of losing candy, the pain of taking candy … and then, the pain of holding this information and feeling bad about it.

FLIGHT PLANS

Consider the effects of *not* confessing:

- How do you think Pete's life would have played out if he had kept this story inside himself?
- How would the memory of that night have affected Hobo if Yoda never came forward?
- Is there a rock in your life that could be moved by confessing to a trusted person? No one could imagine how God would work this out—but He did. Will you allow him to work on some of the seemingly impossible life situations you are in?

THE VOICEMAIL FROM HELL

This is a very personal story about avoiding the rocks and how you can only keep stuff hidden away until they surface. For me, the turning point came with a little jab that you might expect from a worried mom.

"You drink too much," she said.

First, what you need to know is this was *my* mom. Second, she doesn't normally lean into saying really hard things like that. Third, she loves wine, too, so ... what the heck?!

However, when it's my mom, I pay attention. I log it into my brain. But still, I have to groan and protest a little, "Oh, Mom, *please* ..."

Five or six months after that exchange, Marni and I moved into a new neighborhood in San Diego. Maybe you're like this, too: whenever I have moved somewhere new, I try to see myself through the eyes of my new neighbors. It's not just about being extra careful to make sure the lawn is kept up and the noise level down. I'm also aware of how I'm coming across as a human being. Am I living up to what my new neighbors know—or think they know—about me? I'm always conscious that I worked for Young Life, and my new neighbors will be watching (whether they agree with my beliefs or not) to see whether I live up to my Christian values.

Talk about living up to your values. First and foremost, you need to stay accountable to the people you love. At regular intervals (I mentioned this in an earlier chapter), our Covenant group gives our spouses and kids a survey to fill out that asks: How am I doing as a husband? A father? A friend?

Anyway, at some point after we moved into our new neighborhood, it occurred to me that because of a lot of stress, I forgot to get the last survey to Marni.

Or maybe I didn't want to. Okay, I may have been a little uneasy about what my wife thought about me, too. In fact (I'll be honest), I didn't know what she was going to say, but that year, I felt very vulnerable. Whatever she had for me, honestly, I didn't want to hear it.

All these things were lurking in the back of my brain when I went to Palm Desert for the annual Covenant Weekend. One of our exercises during those meetings is to sit in the "yellow chair" and individually share our intentions, hopes and dreams for the coming year. Part of the process is to confess (there's that word again) our vulnerabilities and fears. How have we measured up since we last came together?

This isn't about confessing into the air or spilling your heart to strangers. The point of this confession is to *share,* and that doesn't just go one way. We share with *each other.* That brings accountability. I have the extra blessing of having a very good friend, Jamie, who's in the covenant group with me. So, I knew without a shadow of a doubt that I was with people who supported me, and they felt the same.

So, I'm halfway through my forty-five minutes of sharing, and my phone starts vibrating. It's Marni. I'm not going to say, "Hey, guys, hold on," so I just let it go to voicemail and complete my sharing. We take a break after that, and we all go outside to stretch our legs, get a cup of coffee, some fresh air.

I walk outside to catch up on Marni's voicemail, and what I hear is unnerving: *"Hey, I hope you haven't shared yet because I wanted to share some things with you. I know you're going to hate this, but I got to tell you I think you should take a break from alcohol. I know you're probably mad at me, but ..."*

I stared at my phone. This wasn't what I was expecting. And it wasn't over.

"By the way, on the off chance that you don't share this, I am also leaving the same voicemail for Jamie."

I turned, and there was Jamie, standing directly across the street. It was a moment that had to be arranged by God because, at that very moment, Jamie had his phone to his ear, and he was staring right at me with laser eyes. I knew he was hearing from Marni just the moment I heard from her. Marni signed off her voicemail to me, saying, *"This is what the Lord told me."*

She had to bring the Lord into it! Actually, her last words stoked my courage. In her voicemail, everything finally came together as one message—my mom's warning, my recent self-isolating behavior, that vague sense I was avoiding important truths. I can't tell you how long I lingered outside, trying to figure out what I was going to say, but when I finally walked in for the next covenant session, I knew what I had to do. "I need five more minutes," I told the group.

Hard as it was (and I'm not pretending it was an instant revelation of light and grace—that came later), I told the group that Marni was concerned about me, and I told them why.

"My wife believes I'm drinking too much," I said. "Besides being the love of my life, I respect Marni's wisdom and judgment. The Lord put her in my life not just for my happiness but to kick my butt when I need it. And I need it now."

That was twelve years ago, and I haven't had a drink since. Ever since that day, I've thought of Marni's message as "the voicemail from hell" because it was as if she was watching me from the sidelines of hell, warning me, calling me back, even as I inched farther away from her and everything that was important to me.

I never thought of drinking as an addiction, and I never craved it. I only drank with my friends and in party situations, so the habit was so gradual, but if Marni hadn't noticed (along with my mom), who knows how far I would have slipped down the path? One DUI on the way home from a party, and I would have lost my job.

But besides the public shame and the embarrassment, I would have scandalized the young people who had put all their trust in me. Just one incident with alcohol would have destroyed every principle I had built my life on and believed in for over a lifetime. So, for me, alcohol wasn't about addiction. For me, it was a matter of *account-ability.* I needed to be fully present all the time and *fully accountable* to every person and every young person in my life.

Marni only asked me to take a break from drinking, but I guess I can't do anything halfway. When the truth hit me that day, I knew I was done with alcohol, period, and it's been the greatest freedom I've ever experienced. Don't get me wrong—I understand the enjoyment that comes from alcohol. That's great. We have wine at our house, and when you're my guest, I'm going to offer you a glass of wine. I'm not opposed to drinking at all.

I just don't drink because, for me, it was one of those hidden rocks that needed clearing out; otherwise (and who knows when), it could have wrecked my life.

FLIGHT PLANS

Arrange a quiet time with the most trusted person in your life. Ask: "Have I been fully accountable to you? Have I created hurts or worries that you want to talk about?" Give people who know you best the freedom to give input into your life.

Is there anything that the evil one could use to "take you out?" Disqualify you?

PART III:
INSIDE THE ROPES

....

If you want deeper, more meaningful relationships, don't keep people on the edges of your life. Invite them inside the ropes, where you really live!

"JUST GO"

learned this through a "last minute" idea that I didn't like hearing. (That's me—"Mr. Let Me Think About It Some More.") Ask my wife. Marni knows that when it comes to letting something spontaneous happen, I'm that wet-blanket guy who can't get excited until I know the overall plan. Marni can roll with anything. But me? Pitch a sudden change of plans my way, and I'll drive all of you "carefree types" crazy with a hundred reasons why it's a bad idea.

So, thank you, Lord, for making me listen to my wife on (of all weekends) Mother's Day weekend, 2002. The lesson I learned didn't make me more spontaneous—I'll probably never get *there*—but it taught me so many profound lessons about life that I'm drawing from them to this day.

Marni kicked me into gear that Saturday morning as I was cleaning out the garage. As inspiration for my task, I was also listening to the golf scores coming in from the Byron Nelson Golf Tournament in Dallas. One of the young guys on the leaderboard was a close friend of ours, Ben Crane, and he was coming up in the ranks. He had turned pro in 1999, and this was his first year on the PGA tour. He hoped I would come to Dallas (four hours away) to watch him play.

But, hey, this is garage cleaning weekend! Besides, we had our two-year-old, Hudson, to chase after and a big Mother's Day event at our church the next day. In between shoving boxes around in the garage, I was staying close to the golf channel and the amazing story that was emerging. By noon, our friend, Ben Crane, had moved to sixth place on the leaderboard! This was the best he had ever played since turning pro.

At some point, Marni appeared like a vision between the pile of boxes. She had that steely-eyed, take-no-prisoners look on her face that I'd seen many times before: She was about to push me around.

"I think you should go," she said firmly.

I'll spare you my resistance moves—Marni won. Less than an hour later, I was on my way to the airport with a hastily booked ticket waiting for me there, and thinking, "This is crazy!" But, in spite of myself, even *I* could see the fun of it.

I got to the golf course, the Four Seasons in Dallas, picked up the tickets that Ben had already reserved for me (still hoping that I'd come), and waded into the thick crowd. When I looked up at the Jumbotron, it confirmed that I had done the right thing by coming to support my friend—Ben was now in third place! It was his first year on the PGA tour card, and I could hear the buzz in the crowd, "Who's this Crane?" I wanted to stop in the middle of these people and say, "I know him! He's my friend!" Instead, I smiled and wondered what we'd do for dinner.

At the 18th hole, Ben and I smacked into each other as he was coming out of the scoring tent. His first words made me glad all over again that Marni had won the day.

"Hey, buddy! You made it!" he shouted. (Of course, he had no idea just how last-minute the "you-made-it!" was.) That night, we had dinner, and Ben forbade any talk about golf—he didn't even want to know where he was in the standings. That didn't stop me from being excited; Ben was playing the next day with one of the biggest names on the tour—"The Big Easy" himself, Ernie Els.

The next day, when we got up, I saw a focus in Ben that I had never seen before. For breakfast, I had a chocolate doughnut. Ben had an organic salad. After breakfast, we went to a quiet place for prayer and fellowship. We read Philippians 2:5: *"In your relationships with one another, have the same mindset as Christ Jesus."* The passage goes on to say that Christ did not use his equality with God to his own advantage; He took on servanthood and humbled himself. Quite a lesson for Ben and me on a day when we were both surrounded, each in our own way, by adoring crowds.

Given all that was happening to him, I was impressed by where Ben was in his life. He was hovering at the start of fame and success, but more than ever, he was healthy, focused, and deeply spiritual. That morning, we ate, we prayed, and then Ben got up humbly to go to work. He was one of the top three players in the tournament; he was playing with golf great Ernie Els, but he understood that he still had to pack his bags, pay his hotel bill, and charge his big, first-generation cellphone.

We arrived at the course together, but at the gate, we had to say goodbye. "Good luck, my friend, and God bless," I said. Ben went inside the ropes, and I watched him lope away into the players' tent. That's when it hit me with a tinge of wistfulness (I'm being honest here) how much I was *outside* the ropes.

But still, I was *there*. Complaining was the last thing on my mind. And what a day it was! Ben was playing with a popular veteran champion, Ernie Els, so the gallery was packed. I kept hearing a buzz all around me, "Who's this Ben Crane? Where's he from?"

Ben was playing great golf. Heck, so was Ernie! I'll never forget the moment Ernie got a hole-in-one on a back nine par 3, and I was thinking, "How does Ben compose himself after that?" I looked for Ben's reaction, and it was like he was a fan. He was high-fiving Ernie and pounding his fist heavenwards, as overjoyed as if he had sunk the "ace" himself.

Between the 15th and 16th holes, I called Marni, who had been watching the match on TV. "Can you believe it!" she crowed.

Then Marni said the coolest thing a wife could say on a Mother's Day when you're not there with her but whooping it up by yourself at a PGA golf tournament:

"This is the most exciting thing I have ever watched on TV! My heart is pounding," she said, and then she added the sweetest words ever, "I'm so glad you're there." "Me, too," I whispered back. (God bless my spontaneously minded wife.)

"I'll call you later; sure do love you!" I signed off and headed for the 16th hole. I can only tell you that what followed was a blur. There were amazing shots, towering bleachers of appreciative fans, and a crowd on every green, packed twenty-five deep. Best of all, Ben had settled into his sweet spot—all day long, he was in the running for first place. In the end, he placed an amazing second behind Shigeki Maruyama and won $518,000. It was Ben's biggest payday yet, his best finish in a PGA tournament, and his name was the buzz of the golf world.

As for me, I was as exhilarated and exhausted as if I had been on the leaderboard myself. I slogged through the crowds, found my suitcase in the "will call" tent, and arranged for a taxi. All the while, my heart was bursting with love for my wife, pride for my friend, and amazement at these *spontaneously* perfect two days. As I pushed through the crowd, I only wished I could catch Ben's attention one last time to mouth the words, "Great job! I will call you!" The reality was I was just another guy in my late thirties, wearing beige shorts and a golf hat, struggling through a crowd of 7,000 people.

As I approached the back side of the scoring tent, just off the 18th hole, Ben came around the corner. From forty yards away, with a thousand heads between us, his eyes fastened miraculously on mine. At that moment, I heard him yell out to the security guards, "Hey, you see that guy? I want him inside the ropes!"

I had to look around. Was Ben Crane, the newest sensation on the PGA tour, talking about *me?*

At that moment, I felt the same way I did when Kathy K. asked me to slow dance in the seventh grade. It was like the day I saw my name on a list outside Coach Hoffert's office door, which meant I had made the junior high basketball team.

The tournament handlers charged forward, took my arm, and escorted me through the crowd. I could feel hundreds of eyes suddenly glomming onto *me.* I felt a strange mixture of pride and humility wrestling around in me, and both emotions were fighting for the top spot.

The bottom line was, for the first time in my life, I knew the experience of moving from my ordinary place in the world to "inside the ropes." It's a kind of magical boundary that separates the expected from the unimaginable. Until you've gone from one to the other, you can't know what it's like. You *think* you know—but you don't.

Myself, Marni, Hudson, Ben Crane after he won Torrey Pines

Me caddying at Augusta

Let me try to explain. I had spent roughly forty-eight hours at the side of my friend, but it was only when I was invited *inside the ropes* that I saw the true reality of Ben's world. To my amazement, once inside, some little kids rushed up to me, waving black magic markers and clamoring for my signature on their golf caps! Maybe they thought I was Stewart Cink, one of the other young pros on the tour. Mind boggled, I actually signed a few autographs (scribbling my own name, of course). Without even trying, I had turned into a celebrity just by being *with* a celebrity.

What a gift to be there! With me just off camera, Ben did a flood of interviews—with the Golf Channel, with ESPN, with PGATOUR. com. In just two days, everybody in the crowd had come to know the name "Ben Crane."

As I stood there, I had to marvel at what brought me there. Most of all, I was grateful to Marni, my "spontaneous spouse," who had said, "Just go!"

On the flight home, I started to muse about the lessons this trip taught me. I decided there are three applications that are truly life-changing—not just for me but for anyone who wants to have a meaningful and purpose-filled life.

The first lesson is to realize that, ultimately, we are being invited "inside the ropes" when we make the decision to give our life to Jesus Christ. This is truly, and literally, a life and death decision to come inside the ropes.

The second lesson is that we should recognize that those of us who are already inside the ropes have not only a privilege but an obligation to invite *others* inside (like Ben invited me).

The third lesson is to be watchful because someday, each of us will have the ultimate "inside the ropes" experience. That will be the day we cross the line from this life to eternal life. When we finally see what it's like "on the other side," we will understand why living a good life is so important because it determines whether we'll be invited inside eternal happiness—or not.

Each of us must make these life-changing decisions for ourselves. For me, I really began to "get it" a few weeks later during an evening meet at a camp where I was serving. It was the moment some worship songs were being played on guitar, and I was standing there, taking in the summer evening, the sights, the sounds. I sensed many areas of my life coming together.

I remember thinking... is Jesus Lord of my life? Am I different than all of my neighbors who don't profess a faith? What would it look like to take a step forward... His words were both simple and powerful: *"I want you inside the ropes!"*

I looked around. Was everyone at this camp having the same sensation, the same feeling, the same call?

Maybe you are a believer, too, but somehow, in the commotion of daily life, in the race to make money, to get ahead, maybe you've gotten a little off track. It's not that you're doing anything terrible—you're going to work, raising your kids, and being good to your family.

Yet, somewhere in this mix, you have a sense you're just shoving boxes around in the garage. You need someone to do for you what Marni did for me when she said, *"Just go!"*

These are the words that the world will never tell you. Your kids won't tell you, either. That's because these are the words that never seem to hit at the right time—not with the garage in chaos, the taxes that need paying, the bathroom remodel half done, the books unread, the gym membership unused. No, there's never really a good time to *"Just go!"*

Well, I'm here to tell you—*Just go!* Take your bible, take a journal, or take nothing at all. Go to a park, go to a coffee shop, go on a walk. Just go! Don't worry about what you'll do when you get there. You've already done what I did—dropped the boxes in the garage and got on a plane, so to speak. Now, let God do the rest. It is different inside the ropes! Jesus left us with his Holy Spirit to guide us. He's the one who beckoned to you through the crowds and invited you by name—"I want YOU inside the ropes!"

As I continued to reflect, the next steps became so simple and so clear: once you're inside, *you must invite others* to come inside. That's what Ben did! He had received an awesome gift from God to use his brains, coordination, and athleticism to build a great golfing career. But he didn't just keep his God-given talent to himself—he is using his gift to invite others inside to enhance God's kingdom.

I've watched myself as Ben lifted the ropes—not just for me—but for someone else.

One of my co-workers in Houston has a son, Larry, who has Type 1 diabetes, a serious disease. Larry is a great kid, and he loves golf. Pretty much the highlight of Larry's life was the day he was able to meet Ben Crane through our connections. He had been following Ben's career ever since. One year after Ben made his mark at the Byron Nelson tournament, Larry and his dad were able to catch up with Ben at the Shell Houston Open. Every day, this young man and his father went to the tournament, and at the end of every day, they would wait outside the scoring tent, hoping for a handshake or an autograph, just something that showed Ben remembered them.

So, *did* Ben remember? One day, shortly after the Houston tournament wrapped up, Ben and his wife, Heather, shipped a brand-new set of golf clubs and a golf bag to the family home. The gift card was addressed to "Little Larry."

In one simple gesture, a by-then-famous golfer invited a small boy to join the insiders. He's well beyond the age of nine now, but Larry still practices his golf swings every day and tells people that his reason for following the game is to be "just like Ben."

We all have the power to enrich not only our lives but the lives of others. The first step is to get moving—Just go! Look for the "spontaneous Marni" in your life—that person who will kick you in the backside, get you off the couch, and out of the garage. Until you do that, you'll never get anywhere near the insider's circle. It doesn't matter if you're already there or you want to be. God expects you to act.

FLIGHT PLANS

The ultimate insider is Jesus Christ. He doesn't just want to invite us inside the ropes; He wants us to bring others along too! How can we do that? Well, first look at how Jesus invited Peter into His life—everlasting life. Jesus did it using three very simple methods that could be called a NAP. Notice, Ask, and Push-out -- but Jesus used these simple principles to <u>energize</u> relationships—to go deep into a person's life and transform it from within.

How? He **noticed**, He **asked**, and **He pushed out:**

He **noticed** Peter's boat along the shore. (Imagine how awe-inspiring this must have been for Peter! How many other boats could Jesus have picked out besides his?)

He **asked** Peter to push out from shore. Peter was an expert boatman and fisherman; don't you think he was excited and awed to be tagged for a ride by a famous rabbi (which is all he knew about Jesus at the time)? Don't you think Jesus asked him questions about the boat, the best fishing weather, and what made a good haul at that time of year? <u>There is great power in asking people questions about their lives.</u>

Finally, Jesus **pushed out** into Peter's life by stepping onto the boat and beginning to share in Peter's experiences as a fisherman.

Notice. Ask. Push-out.

Notice: How many people did you physically see today? (Maybe you saw them only for an instant as you bought coffee or picked up your dry cleaning. Or maybe it's someone you see often but in a casual way.) How would you describe them?

Ask: Many people dread meeting strangers. I guarantee you'll have fun meeting strangers if you just remember to *ask*. If you could pull one of those people aside for a few moments, what would you want to ask them about their lives? You might be surprised at how much people want to open up: Does your job make you happy today? Could you use some supportive words or an encouraging prayer? Who's at home waiting for you tonight?

The list is endless: Who's your best friend? What's the hardest thing you're facing in your life right now? What would you like to be remembered for? If I gave you $100 right now, what would you do with it? Who are the significant people in your life right now?

Pushed out: Ask to go aboard—see another person's life from the inside. Think of the ways you can safely board someone else's life. Have a meal together. Offer to help with a home project (one of my favorites, of course, cleaning out the garage!). If they wonder why you're being so helpful, just tell them, "I'm hoping we can get to know each other better, and I think a good afternoon of cleaning is a good way to do it." Invite them to church. Invite them to a meal. Your goal is to build a relationship. You're offering them the opportunity to come inside the ropes.

LILLIAN

Pry open your heart. Look around. I bet somebody out there needs you to invite them—even push them—inside the ropes and into the light.

I'll be honest with you—I'm often slow to take that advice myself. The year Lillian joined our weeklong camp, it made people nervous. Lillian was in a wheelchair, and she wore very thick lensed glasses, so when you looked straight into her eyes, her eyes were magnified, and she had beautiful eyes at that! Of course, very few kids looked into her eyes. In fact, they found it hard to look at Lillian at all. Even worse, Lillian couldn't really talk. Everything she said was garbled and amounted to a bunch of "ahhhs," which also made people nervous. Yes, we all had to adjust to Lillian.

It wasn't easy to enter her world. I learned that personally on the last day of camp. We always end the week with a grand finale celebration, topped by a personal declaration of faith. We base our declaration on Psalm 107:2, which tells us that the redeemed of the Lord should say so out loud. So, we do! At the end of the third verse, my role is to stand up before the crowd and announce, "If you have made a decision to follow Jesus this week, please stand up!" Then I take a microphone in the crowd, and each person stands up to give a one-sentence testimonial of faith.

What I forgot was that Lillian couldn't stand up. I only realized that as I started around the crowd, passing the microphone around to each kid standing. My heart started sinking as I approached Lillian. There she was, standing between the two leaders that brought her, holding up up out of her wheelchair so she could be standing, like I asked.

I'll never forget how Lillian looked up at me from her wheelchair, I could tell how proud she was. (It was so quiet, it felt like you could hear the field mice breathing outside.) Then she said, "My name is Lillian, and I invited God into my life this week." That one sentence took her about a minute to say. At the end of her faith declaration, the room erupted in applause, and her smile lit up the crowd brighter than sunshine. I was humbled by this young woman's bravery and grace, and I prayed that she would find her place in life.

What do you know—the next summer, Lillian was back again! This time, she was on the work crew. She came back to serve. But as a camp director, I was responsible for the kids' well-being, so my concern was, what in the world is Lillian going to do? At that time, we had never had a kid with a disability on the work crew before. We decided to put her in the laundry. When the clean towels came down to be folded, Lillian was there every day to make the last fold. She did great. Every morning, I would get up early for my coffee, but I never beat Lillian to the sunrise. Lillian was always up before any of us. By the time we got to breakfast, Lillian was sitting in her chair underneath a huge shade tree, reading her Bible. She always greeted us with the sweetest smile.

Then came the end of the month. Every session, as the month winds down, the kids always get a little squirrely; it's hard for them to think about saying goodbye to their new friends, and they don't want the camp experience to end. So, we give the kids some latitude to break loose with their emotions. On one of the final nights, we arrange a great party experience for them at a spot called Mill Pond, the equivalent of a two-block walk past the lodge down a rocky hiking trail. Waiting for them at the Mill Pond is memorable—their favorite music is blaring away, Kool-Aid is flowing, and everywhere they look are endless slices of pepperoni pizza.

Best of all, as they come to the end of the trail, right in front of them, breaking out from the dark, is a lighted dance floor. It's magical. As the kids reach the blaze of light, you can hear the bursts of surprise and wonder. The dancing starts, the pizza flows, and even we adults can get a little emotional (though we try to hide it) on this special last night of celebration.

As fun as it is, my role as a camp director is to stay alert and keep my eyes roaming over the landscape like a searchlight, looking for anything, anyone, that needs help. That night, I suddenly noticed a shadowy silhouette about fifty yards outside the circle of dancing lights. It was Lillian! Immersed in all the teenage rituals that mark the end of summer—the tears, the heart-wrenching goodbyes, the crazy letting loose for the last time—everybody had forgotten Lillian. So, she had taken off on her own, barreling over the rough terrain in her motorized chair, determined to get to the Mill Pond. In the dark, her chair got stuck in the rocks and sand.

"Hey, guys, Lillian needs help!" Instantly, as soon as the rallying cry went up, everything changed—the kids dashed from the dance floor that was lit up with spotlights and headed into the dark toward Lillian. Pretty soon, a twenty kids were all around her, each

123

doing what they could to push her heavy chair, each of them pushing Lillian into the light.

Finally, the crowd got Lillian and her chair to the center of "party central"—the lighted dance floor. As soon as Lillian reached that pool of light, other kids rushed forward to share with her some pizza and punch. I have a picture of three of us gathering around Lillian's chair; she's got some pasta sauce smeared on the side of her face and the happiest look ever. That night, Lillian had the time of her life— and so did the other kids. Just not exactly in the way they expected.

Many years ago, a remarkable man, Sam Shoemaker, wrote a poem that became the title for a biography about his life called *I Stand at the Door*. Sam Shoemaker was an Episcopal priest and co-founder of Alcoholics Anonymous, and he knew better than most that we are all accountable to each other and we must look out for each other. Shoemaker's poem is long and worth reading in its entirety. It's about the man who stands by the door, waiting to bring others in from the dark—whether it's physical disability, or loneliness, or alcoholism: "I stand by the door," he wrote: *"The most tremendous thing in the world is for men to find that door—the door to God ..."*

"But I wish they wouldn't forget how it was
Before they got in. Then they would be able to help
The people who have not yet found the door,
Or the people who want to run away again from God."

Lillian was stuck in the dark because of her disability. And the rest of us were all blinded by the light of the dance floor, at least for a time. As Sam Shoemaker knows, it's easy to forget what it's like to be outside, not knowing how to get into the light, onto the dance floor! Not everyone can get there on their own, whether it's friendship or a relationship with God. If we are honest, don't we all get stuck somewhere, sometime, in our lives?

The rest of us need to be alert to see who needs help getting inside the ropes and into the light.

FLIGHT PLANS

Who in your life right now is stuck ... stuck in the dark?

What do you love and experience on the dance floor and in the light?

When you step off the dance floor, as you scan the horizon of your life, who are you seeing that needs an invitation?

GREG'S LAST PROM

When I was a student teacher, one of my sophomore students was a nice kid named Greg Baker. Everybody liked Greg. He had a determined look in his eye, like he wanted everybody to know he wasn't going to put up with BS from anybody. And Greg had a lot to put up with—he had muscular dystrophy. From the neck down, Greg was pretty much immobile.

I got to know Greg because of the elevator. It was one of those complicated, old-fashioned elevators with a cage inside the outer two doors. First, the doors slide open, left and right, and then the cage opens, bottom to top. It was a challenge for us all.

For Greg, the elevator wasn't just a challenge; it was impossible. My classroom was on the second floor, next to the elevator, so I was the guy who met Greg and maneuvered his wheelchair in and out of the elevator. With the wheelchair, the cramped doors, and the cage rolling up and down—it was like maneuvering in and out of a giant tin can! You get to know somebody in that kind of circumstance; we both had to struggle, each in our own way, with this heavy, creaky piece of machinery. Both of us needed patience and humor every single time.

From the ancient elevator to a top education, Greg took on every challenge. He could do some writing, and he was memorable for scoring a perfect score on the SAT—1600 out of 1600. I remember thinking, "Whoa, who is this kid?" Greg handled the sound system at the track meets, and he was the announcer for the school's sports events. This was a kid who wasn't going to let anything stop him.

When my student teaching ended, I took a staff job with Young Life, but I still had ties to the high school. I was there to see the kids transform from gangly, 14-year-old teens to maturing young men and women.

But the most dramatic change was in Greg.

There's no other way to put it—Greg's system was shutting down. One of the many heartbreaking outcomes of his struggle was that he had worked exceptionally hard to win a college scholarship, and he got one. But by the time his accomplishment was announced, he had already decided to turn it down. He knew his time was short.

Senior year came in a flash. Then it was over. By spring, the kids felt an urgency to pack everything into the last few weeks: "*This is our last exam ... our last baseball game ... our last prom ...*"

I happened to be a chaperone at the senior prom that year. It was held in a huge ballroom at the Elks Club, probably the fanciest prom setting these kids had experienced up to then. My job was to guard one of the exit doors. For safety reasons, I had to make sure that once the prom started, nobody could come in or go out. Well, my job was easy because nobody was coming near me *or* the exit door! Usually, the students liked coming over to chat with us, except on prom night. That night, we adults didn't exist. The young people were in their own world.

So, I just stood there in the dark, a few feet away from the swirling lights on the dance floor and watched all those nice kids trying their darnedest to act grown up. Guys who were smooth athletes on the basketball court shuffled their feet like bashful youngsters as they made small talk with their dates. (I remember those days!) Girls who were serious students by day looked on prom night like movie stars, with their dramatic makeup and their hair piled, Greek goddess style, on top of their heads. The prom was memorable, exciting, and awkward all at the same time. Senior prom night is an experience that makes young people especially eager to reach adulthood, and on that night, adulthood seems almost close enough to touch.

About an hour into the prom, I saw six students, three couples, break away from the dance floor and go over to talk to the principal. These three couples were among the smartest and most popular kids at school. I couldn't help but be curious as I watched them surround the principal, obviously excited and trying to convince him of something. Whatever they said, suddenly, they were gone—the three couples just disappeared from the ballroom. This was a first. It was a firm rule; once at prom, you could not leave prom. Ever.

Here's what none of us knew at the time. A few miles away, Greg Baker was doing what he did every Saturday night: he was watching TV with his parents. Really, there was nowhere for him to go because he was pretty much trapped in the wheelchair. It was as bulky as a truck engine, with a big battery pack attached, and to get him in and out of the family van was a real production. So, he never went anywhere unless he had to, and because of all the complications, he never went anywhere he wasn't expected.

Go to prom? He didn't even bother to ask his mom. Actually, he didn't even want to think about it. Are you kidding? What could *he* do at prom? All the other kids would be there with their dates. There would be dancing. He'd just be in the way.

That night, there was a knock on the Baker family's front door. When Mrs. Baker opened the door, six young people, decked out in tuxes and long dresses, burst into the living room.

"You're coming to prom!" It was a command, not a request. Greg looked up from his chair, struggling to say something. (Five minutes earlier, he was watching a Saturday night TV variety show. Now, six of the most popular kids at school were standing in his living room, surrounding him in a cloud of perfume and aftershave!)

Pretty much all he could manage, over and over again, was, "No ... I ... can't."

"This is your senior year! You've *got* to come!" They were relentless. They wore him down. His protests got fainter. Finally, with the help of his mom, the girls pinned a clip-on tie on Greg's shirt, and someone threw a jacket around his shoulders.

Less than an hour after they left, the group was back at the Elks Club, and Greg Baker was with them. As they started wheeling him into the ballroom and closer to the light of the dance floor, you could see more and more people in the crowd start to notice. The party buzz slowly morphed from a noisy din to a mass greeting:

"It's Greg! It's Greg Baker!"

Suddenly, as Greg's wheelchair fully entered the light of the dance floor, everybody saw at once what was happening. That's when the room erupted. The cheering, the clapping—it was so loud, you could actually feel an energy force push its way through the ballroom. It felt like a wind blast. I think I finally knew what the phrase meant, "shaking the rafters."

For the rest of the night, Greg was the king of the prom. He was pushed around the dance floor by gorgeous young ladies in sparkling gowns, and the guys fought each other to refill his refreshments. Greg's body was worn out, but that night, he was happy.

The prom was on May 25. Greg Baker died on June 25. This happened more than thirty years ago, but I still remember that young man being spun around on the dance floor, motionless in his wheelchair but with a grin on his face and surrounded by friends.

To this day, I also remember those young men and women who did a rare thing. At a time when they were on top of the world and had everything going for them, they thought beyond their own happiness to someone else. They weren't even sure they could do it—they knew the rule, "no leaving prom after it starts"—but they convinced "the powers that be" anyway. Then, they had to convince a tired and dying young man that he was worth having around. They *wanted* him there—they *wanted* to be with him. And they wouldn't take "no" for an answer.

Generosity unleashes an amazing, unforgettable power that can last a lifetime. In fact, the six kids who "kidnapped" Greg Baker, who brought him *inside the ropes*, have never forgotten their last prom. Greg's parents haven't forgotten what happened that night, and obviously, neither have I.

We can only guess what memories Greg had held close during his last month on earth. Somehow, I think Greg's last prom might have been one of those memories. He was there because his friends saw him on the outside, and they opened the door to let him in.

"I stand by the door.
I neither go too far in, nor stay too far out.
The door is the most important door in the world—
It is the door through which men walk when they find God."
—Sam Shoemaker

FLIGHT PLANS

Because some young people cared, the rest of us learned an unforgettable lesson:

- When did you last "open the door" for someone?
- Can you think of a time someone "stood at the door" for you?
- Who do you need to remember today?
- Who is struggling or has some hard circumstances going on?
- Reach out? Call? Text? Note?
- "I see you" is a powerful comment.

PART IV:
BELIEVE IN PEOPLE

Believe in people, even the hopeless ones.

THE CUSSER

A good woman stood at her sink, washing dishes. Outside her window, a kid was making it really hard to enjoy her home. From that odd combination of circumstances, God did something amazing.

First, about the kid. He was probably a 6thgrader, always was at the park playing hoops, and had a pretty good size attitude, both confidence, competitiveness, and anger. He and his buddies were obsessed with basketball and constantly setting up games on this court. Unfortunately for the neighbor lady, she couldn't avoid his obsession because her house backed up against the basketball court. As she stood at her sink washing dishes, all she'd hear outside her window was the angry-sounding pound, pound, pound of a basketball on concrete.

But something else was even harder on her ears.

The kid was a cusser. He used words that she hadn't heard since ... well, she had *never* heard those words! This kid and his friends were passionate kids for sure, and she could take it all in from her kitchen window. This kid might have been a cusser, but she could also tell by the kids he was with and the clothes he was wearing, he came from a good home. Probably from the street not far from this court – which was full of kids all around the same age.

How she wanted to open her windows and just breathe in the fresh spring air! She knew the birds were singing again after a hard winter, but she couldn't hear them. All she could hear was the pound, pound, pound of a basketball on concrete, the kids passionate fighting, and of course, the "cusser" as she liked to call him.

But if she couldn't enjoy a beautiful spring day, there was still one thing she *could* do: She could pray for him.

So, that's what she did. She stood at her kitchen sink and prayed for that kid whose heart was burdened who desperately needed the Lord. She didn't know his name, so she prayed for, "The Cusser." Honestly, things changed for her a bit. She started to look forward to the kids being on the court, and even hearing some of the arguing. It was a all a reminder to pray for her new friend, "The Cusser." "The Prayer" chose to *stand in the gap* for a kid she didn't even know.

At the same time, the woman was praying for someone she didn't know; I was out there in the world and needed *lots* of prayers. I was lost, making poor choices, and rushing toward life in all the wrong directions. None of those directions pointed toward Jesus because no one had pointed him out to me. But you know what? Prayer was working for me, even though I didn't know it.

Everything came together at an important Young Life banquet, a fundraising dinner for three hundred supporters. Talk about intimidating! I had only met the Lord a few months before, and this was one of my first Young Life events. My buddies and I were in charge of serving dinner to the guests. In the middle of bringing out the bread, pouring the iced tea, and balancing spaghetti plates, one of the leaders stood up and announced that when everyone was served, each of us kids should pick one of the fifty tables set up around the room, and join the adults there. Then, he told the audience, "Invite the young person at your table to share their testimony."

Testimony? I didn't even know what a testimony was, much less that I had one. Desperate, I headed for one of the fifty tables—any table. Okay, this table! Ten adults were already seated. I just stood there, facing them, not knowing what else to do. It felt like twenty eyes were just staring at me. Then somebody said, "Okay, young man, thanks for joining us! We're interested in hearing your testimony."

I decided to be honest about it. "I'm sorry, I don't even know what a testimony is." For a kid on the hot seat, the next thing that happened was like a miracle because the adults started helping me out with their own questions: "How did you get involved in Young Life? What are your interests? Where do you go to school?" With their encouragement, I started bumbling my way through, and they seemed to like what I had to say. By the end, I thought it went pretty well.

So, the banquet was winding down, and all of us, the work crew for the night, were in charge of cleaning up. I was busy shoving stuff in trash bins and garbage cans and doing my thing when a woman came up to me.

"Excuse me, may I talk to you for a minute?"

"Sure," I said.

"I was at your table tonight, and I'm wondering if I can ask you a few questions?"

"Oh sure, absolutely!" (Hey, I got through my first testimony; I guess I can handle a few more questions.)

The nice lady asks me where I grew up. When I said, "Holmes Court," her face lit up as if I had confirmed something. "That's close to Hillandale Park, isn't it?" she asked, and when I said, "Yeah," she replied, "Did you ever play basketball at Hillendale Park?"

"Gosh, all the time!"

"I knew it! I knew I recognized you! I'm sorry for asking this," the lady said, "but did you used to cuss a lot?"

Yes, that's right. I'm the cusser. Standing in front of that nice lady, all I wanted to do was crawl into the trash bin along with all the used-up cups and smeared paper plates. Humiliated and embarrassed—all I could think to stammer out was, "Do you know my mom?" She said, no, "I don't even know your last name." I said, "Okay, well, yeah, as a matter of fact, I'm dealing with the cussing thing, and I'm still working on it."

Instead of looking at me with disgust, the lady looked ecstatic. "I knew it! I knew it!" she said. "My house backs up against the basketball court. I used to stand at my kitchen sink and pray for the cusser. I didn't know your name, but I just knew when you came to my table tonight, I knew that the Lord wanted me to know that my prayers were answered."

For a minute, the lady and I just looked at each other. Each of us was on the other side of the same miracle! I had picked one table out of fifty, and she was at that table because God wanted her to be there. He wanted her to come face to face with the miracle *she* had set in motion years before.

One of the classic books I have enjoyed, *The Intercessor*, is about the life of Rees Howells. In it, there is a moment, "One day Rees noticed a group of intoxicated women and felt a stirring in his heart to pray for the ringleader—a woman of terrible reputation—through to salvation by Christmas Day. During this time, the Holy Spirit made it clear to him that he was to have no contact with her—she was to be won by prayer alone by "binding the strong man," as in Matthew 12:29.

During the weeks of prayer for this woman, God took Rees deeper into the realm of the Spirit and spiritual warfare. As he prayed, he was encouraged to see her getting nearer to God, attending the open-air meeting and then the house meeting. Finally, on Christmas Day, she attended church and, in the middle of the meeting, went down on her knees and cried to God for mercy.

He even said during the service, when she came, it was "not the right setting in the service," as kids were being loud and crying. Yet, it had nothing to do with anything but prayer and believing.

Sure, He could have worked on me alone—and He did—that's why I had joined Young Life. But God is so good that He wanted to do more. He wanted the woman who prayed for me to see the effects right before her eyes.

FLIGHT PLANS

- <u>Will YOU stand in the gap</u> for a lost kid around your life? Or maybe it's a lost family member? Or somebody you know who got off track, who isn't living up to their faith or family? Or maybe—this one is hard—will you stand up for someone you just don't like very much—like a cusser?

- <u>Family prayer is powerful</u>. Gather family around, and ask each one:

    * Who will you stand in the gap for?

    * How can each one of us help?

    * What prayers should we say for this person?

- <u>Ask your family:</u> What prayers have been answered? Who have you helped?

- <u>Who in your life right now is a distraction?</u> They are your version of the cusser.

- <u>Would you consider praying for them, even if you don't know them or might not ever see them again?</u>

LUKE SAVES THE DAY

'm a basketball guy. I love the game. I've played the game, and I believe it's one of those sports that teaches kids how to grow into men. No massive equipment is needed; at entry level, all you need is a ball and a pair of sneakers. Basketball requires individual initiative, teamwork, and decision-making at an incredibly fast pace. A typical play, a winning score, might come as fast as a handshake.

I love this story because our job is to believe in people and what they can do in a split second—even when nobody else believes in them.

I was very psyched to serve as the basketball coach for the rec center that covered our neighborhood in San Diego, called Carmel Mountain Ranch. Just as gratifying as coaching was watching our son, Hudson, grow up from a little guy to become eligible for the team when he turned twelve. By that time, I had been coaching for three or four years, and I knew the drill. It involved taking part in a draft system, just like the pros.

On this particular draft day, I had some steam. I knew the boys I wanted for our team. Like all the coaches, I was familiar with all the kids who had signed up. Sergio, the guy running the draft, introduced the teams and opened the process.

The draft is held privately with just the coaches present. Even though it's held in a cramped little room, you know that somewhere

143

outside that tiny room, huge numbers of kids are waiting to find out if they made a team. As each young man's name is called, the coach declares, out loud, one by one, if he wants that young man for his team. Sure, it's great for a kid when the first coach pipes up—that takes the boy out of contention. He knows he's wanted. But what if more and more coaches pass on a kid? That's the brutal part.

About halfway through the draft, Sergio announces that the next kid up is Luke so-and-so. He goes to the first coach and gives Luke's full name again and waits for the coach's answer. "No," the coach says. He goes to the next coach. "No." Sergio goes to the third coach. "No." So it goes down the line.

No coach wants Luke.

I'm listening to this—I'm the last coach in the line—and I'm thinking, "I know this kid is friends with Hudson ... there are rumors he's hard to work with ... he doesn't listen ... I know he's a rough kid ...."

By the time my turn comes, I know what I want to do, and I say without hesitation, "I will take Luke." I know he comes from a big Greek family—a really fine family, very passionate and fiery and demonstrative (think *My Big Fat Greek Wedding*). I know Luke is passionate and fiery, too, a living ball of emotion. He'll cry if he gets super frustrated. I figure working with him will be kind of like working with a stick of lit dynamite, but I'm willing to take it on.

So, I get my team. We head into the season, and it turns out to be a great one. Never, in all my years of coaching, had we made it to the Carmel Mountain Rec Center playoffs. But that year? We make it all the way to the championship game!

Have you ever noticed that life has a funny symmetry to it, as if God sometimes wants to show His sense of humor? It felt like that to us. First, we made it to the big game for the first time in our history. Second, the opponent we were facing was led by the most obnoxious coach of all. In fact, he was the coach who made a point of shouting out a loud and ringing "NO" when Luke's name came up in the draft. This coach and his team were known for being extremely straitlaced; they were the *righteous* team (and you better not forget it)! After the draft, when all the coaches were standing around discussing our picks, this coach went out of his way to let everybody know (me, especially because I had picked Luke) that the kid was a bad egg, had a bad attitude, and would be nothing but trouble on a team.

Well, how sweet is this? Despite the prediction of the righteous prophet, our team—*with* Luke—made it to the championships! It was a great game, too, because it was a nail-biter that went back and forth the whole game.

I remember it like it was yesterday: With twelve seconds left, we're in trouble. We've probably lost the game. But in the next dozen seconds, a lot happens—a *whole* lot! Our strategy is to purposely foul one of their players, which puts him on the line for a free throw. We're counting on him missing the free throw—and he does.

Now my son, Hudson, has his own shining moment: He gets the rebound, dribbles twice, and looks fast for a teammate who's open. He passes to Luke.

At this point, there are still ten seconds on the clock. Luke dribbles it up the court, crosses to half-court, and still has ten feet to go before he's even to the three-point line. Then he pulls up. From a good thirty-five feet away, he aims, shoots, and swishes it. The ball whistles into the basket like it's magnetized.

Luke! The crowd is going wild because now we're up a point. Luke, true to his reputation, is so overwhelmed that he falls to the ground and starts crying. He forgets there are still six seconds left in the game.

While he's crying, our opponent has the ball—for us, that's not a good place to be—but it turns out not to matter. They come up to shoot, and they miss.

We win the game. The gym erupts in pandemonium; the bleachers are shaking and thundering with hundreds of kids jumping up and down; the place is reverberating with yells and shouts. I turned to a buddy who'd been sitting on the floor because the gym was standing-room-only. My buddy looks at me, shrugs, and then says, with a big grin, "Well, winners win."

I've quoted that line ever since. Isn't it the truth? As I look over, Luke is in the center of a maelstrom, almost lost in a mass of celebrators who are drowning him in hugs and pounding him on the back. And he's still crying.

I thought, is this not faith? Is this not the way the Lord would do it? The kid that nobody wants, the kid who is rejected and scorned, wins the game. On draft day, Luke was scorned by all—when his name was announced, each coach said, "No," "No," "No." One of them capped it by saying "No!" in a loud and jeering voice. But you know what? At that moment, Luke was sharing in a portion of the hurt that Christ felt on the cross when He was jeered and scorned. But God is so good—he wanted Luke to share in the *victory* of the cross, too. Like Christ, the ultimate hero who rescued us from death, Luke saved the day—and ended up the hero.

I love each moment of this story—the moment when we beat that team, the moment when Luke collapses in happy shock, the moment he goes from pariah to hero.

Why? Because our job is to *believe* in people—the people that others disregard! Believe in the underdog and the cusser. Believe in the kid with the bad attitude, that he can turn it around. Believe in the kid who went to rehab. Believe in the family that's separated, but now they're getting back together. The world will never do it, so it's up to us—we have to believe in the cussers and the Lukes of this world, the people the world so often says aren't worth it.

FLIGHT PLANS

- Can you think of someone who you find obnoxious and unbearable? Or maybe annoying? Dull and boring? Invite that person to lunch, call them up, do something to get to know them. I guarantee—something will happen that will surprise you!
- Who is a "Luke" in your world? Make an impact and PICK THEM.

A LOST KID ON A MOUNTAIN

How much is a kid's life worth?

For hundreds of kids and me—one in particular—the answer to that question unfolded at Mount Bachelor, an ancient volcano that rises up a rugged 9,000 feet in Oregon's Cascade Range. Mount Bachelor looks like a mountain should. It's a beautiful A-shape, and in winter, it earns its reputation as one of the top ten ski and snowboard destinations in the country.

As this story unfolds, it's winter 1998, and I'm in charge of taking three hundred kids to Mount Bachelor for a long holiday weekend of skiing and snowboarding. Three hundred kids—that's about seven bus loads.

Now, for those of us in charge, a ski and snowboard day with three hundred kids is enjoyable, but it's not exactly a picnic. It's intense work and a real responsibility to keep track of hundreds of kids, especially making sure they get on and off their assigned bus. By the time it's dark—and that comes early in a northern winter—we need to know each kid is back at the hotel and in line for a hearty spaghetti dinner.

So, now it's the end of day two, and I'm at my usual spot—crunching along in the snow, stopping at each of the seven fume-belching buses, leaning inside the door, holding my roster, and asking each driver if every kid is accounted for. "You got everybody?" "Yes," "Yes," "Yes."

As soon as everybody's confirmed, the bus is free to leave. The process takes a long time—you have to wait for kids who are in the bathroom, searching for a lost ski, a jacket they left on a chair—it might take a couple of hours to round up everybody.

This night, by the time most of the buses have pulled out, it's not just dark; it's brutally cold. Classic frostbite weather. I couldn't be happier to give the okay and watch each bus roll away. But as I look up and down the line, I see Bus 44, the last bus, is still idling. It's so cold the exhaust is billowing out of "44" like a mushroom cloud. I crunch over on the icy snow, lean inside the door, and ask, "Hey, what's going on? You got everybody?" As I do, I see the concern on the driver's face. "We're missing one," he says.

It's now seven o'clock at night, and it's frostbite weather. But that kind of cold is nothing compared to the cold lump of fear that's starting to knit up, stitch by stitch, in my gut. "Who is it?" I ask. "Bryan Halferty," the driver says.

Bryan Halferty! The kid with his name already in lights—the classic "most likely to succeed" kid. Bryan is handsome, happy, and known as a "girl magnet." But for a young man, he is also exceptional because he has learned at a young age to use his natural gifts wisely. In other words, Bryan is a good kid and a nice one. He's responsible, too—the last person you'd expect would keep people waiting.

So, I'm standing on the running board of Bus 44, going through scenarios in my head. Bryan brought a brand-new snowboard on this trip—*I bet he left it somewhere in the lodge, and he's gone to retrieve it.* Wait—this is more likely—*he met a girl on the slopes, and he got on her bus!* I'm almost immediately relieved when I think of that; Bryan is so gregarious, he makes friends so easily, and to the girls, he's already a celebrity. Of course. He's caught up somewhere in a crowd of admirers, and we'll see him back at the hotel.

I assemble our team on our walkie-talkies (remember, this is 1998, still the dark age of technology). "Anybody extra on your bus?" "No. Nobody." Each time, the word comes back like a fresh punch in the gut until, finally, it dawns on me: *We're actually missing a kid.* Before the trip, I had distributed liability and health forms for each young person: *"In case of accident, please call ..." "If hospitalization is required ..."* Those forms were always just pieces of paper, until now.

Sick at heart, I hike up to the lodge to find the Mount Bachelor staff.

"What do I do if I'm missing a kid?" I ask. That starts a whole round of, "Are you sure?" "Have you checked everywhere?" The questions are excruciating because, by then, we *know* we're sure— we've checked every bus, we've checked the hotel where we're staying. Bryan Halferty isn't anywhere.

In a night of unforgettable moments, here's one that stands out. The staff person picks up a phone, but before he dials the number, he turns to me with concern and compassion in his eyes and says, "Okay, I'm going to call search and rescue, but I hope you understand that someone is going to have to pay the bill."

Okay, this is truly a scary moment. It hits me that I have responsibility for somebody's missing child, and at the same time, I'm also agreeing to a huge financial commitment. My mind is racing: *"Oh, my gosh, it's $5,000 an hour to send out the ski patrol ... the snow* *mobiles ... the Saint Bernard dog with the whisky barrel around his neck ... this is a major rescue!"*

Amazing how your mind can race like that. But at the same time, my priorities are never clearer. With zero hesitation, I reply, "Yes, I understand. We'll figure it out."

I swear to you, the guy barely gives the "Okay" on the phone when, out of nowhere, people in orange rescue suits swarm into the lodge like a charging army. Outside, we hear revving snowmobiles. Teams are shouting directions to each other. There's a roar like fifty jet engines going off at once, and then, heading off, they fade into silence. All we can do now is wait.

At one o'clock in the morning, I'm roused from an overstuffed chair where I've been in a nightmarish, ten-minute doze. My team is doing no better—we can't sleep, but exhaustion takes us down for a few minutes at a time until dread and horror jerk us awake again: *Oh my God, one of our young people is missing. Bryan Halferty is missing.*

But now it sounds like a thousand troops are blasting through the lodge door all at once, and their message is sweet: "We have him! He's okay!"

Bryan Halferty is safe, but barely. He was found two and a half miles off the ski run, passed out in a tree well. Whatever accident had taken him down—he couldn't remember anything—that accident had also made off with his brand-new snowboard. He never saw it again. Most seriously, the night was so desperately cold Bryan came close to dying. He had peed himself just trying to stay warm. The rescue team told us, very gravely, that if Bryan had not been found, he would not have made it through the night.

Today, when I tell this story at a banquet, I throw out a challenge to the audience: *"How much is it worth to find a kid?"* Would you authorize us to send out search and rescue if it's *your* kid who is lost? Okay, and if it's somebody else's?

Either way—your kid, my kid—everybody gets it right away. Everybody understands the cost is worth it. *Of course* you send out the rescue team! This expert team found Bryan curled up in a tree well, hidden in pitch-black darkness. The hefty price tag was sacrificial, but it was necessary because nobody but experts could have found him. I believe they were also guided by the Lord because finding Bryan was such a hit-and-miss thing, and his life was in the balance.

There are two postscripts to the story. First, it cost thousands of dollars to find Bryan. In the early days after his rescue, as I concluded his story, I would ask audiences, "Is there a price, a value, on finding a kid? Is $5,000 an hour, or $25,000 to find a kid, too much?"

Well, each time I tell the story of Bryan's rescue, our supporters and benefactors answer me with the same zero hesitation that I had when I authorized the rescue—they step up and cover the cost, and they do it over and over again.

Truth is, since 1998, that rescue bill has been paid more times than I can count, but the story still resonates because there are so many more Bryan's out there who need our help. No, not all of them are lost on a cold mountain in winter; some are lost through drugs, alcohol, or a bad home life. Or even a cusser's bitter heart. There is work to be done every day to save a kid's life.

Now, a postscript to the story. If Bryan had died that night, people would have mourned and wondered what that bright and handsome kid would have done with his life. Thanks to God and the rescue team, we know the answer:

Today, Bryan Halferty is the lead pastor of an exciting and thriving church in Tacoma, Washington. It may not be surprising that the mission of Anchor Church is to welcome the young, the lost, the searching: *"We believe that everyone can belong in a Christ-following community,"* says Anchor's vision statement. *"Seekers, cynics, Christ-followers, and Christ-forgetters. Belief is not a prerequisite for belonging. We will open our arms and our doors to all because we have found that same warmth in the One we follow."*

You can check out Bryan's church at anchortacoma.org, and on the team page, you can see Bryan's photo. I have to smile while looking at it. Bryan is still a handsome guy, and the only thing that looks older and deeper on him isn't wrinkles (he has none); it's the wisdom in his eyes. I have to think that when Bryan prayed about his new church and what he wanted to accomplish for the Lord, he must have thought about his brush with death years before and how he was rescued.

For every person lost—for whatever reason—the stakes are always as high as life and death. Here's how Bryan puts it in his vision statement: *"Our hope is rooted in the One that has defeated death. We won't give up or give in. Even as we struggle, we will hold fast and tight to the Hope-Giver."*

Each of us has such an awesome responsibility to search for the lost person! That's what we did on Mount Bachelor so many years ago. We believed in a lost kid, curled up in a tree well and facing death. We didn't give up, and neither did Bryan. That awful night, hope was there.

FLIGHT PLANS

"Believe in the underdog. Believe in the kid with the bad attitude— that he can turn it around. Believe in the kid who went to rehab. Believe in the family that's separated, but now they're getting back together. Somebody has to believe in the people disregarded by the world. And sometimes, big as an unexpected burst of fireworks, that person can surprise you!"

- Think deeply—ask your family. Gather some good friends around. Somebody knows someone in your neighborhood, your kid's school, your church, who seems lost:
- If it's a kid who's struggling at school, could you be a tutor?
- If it's a rough kid, could you take a small group, introduce yourselves, and ask if you can help? Take him to dinner? Meet his family? Offer to be a mentor?
- If it's a family "down on its luck" (say, in a health or financial crisis), can you offer to run errands once a week? Take up an anonymous donation to help defray expenses, or simply treat the family to a "fun night?"
- Can you pray—like the woman at her kitchen window did? Against all odds—and against her ears—she believed in a cusser, and she prayed for him.

PART VI:
CRAZY PRAYERS

....

We can never figure out God.
He will always be a step ahead of us.

AND THE LORD'S ANSWER IS ...
SOCCER?

If we listen, the Lord has endless ways to tap us on the shoulder to say, "Hey! Pay attention!" I just wasn't expecting a tap while sprawled in the deck chair of a cruise ship. At that moment, I was squinting out to sea, tapping my pen against my private journal, and wondering how to write out the question at the top of my mind.

At this time, I was about ten years into my Young Life ministry and taking a rare vacation. My travel companions were my mother, a very good friend of mine, and his mother. We had been to Bermuda, and now we were bound for home. It was the perfect mix of family and friendship that I needed at that time in my life. It was 1994, and I was young, still single, and tantalized by the next ten years that stretched before me.

It was the last day of the trip, and everybody had scattered to get ready for the big finale celebration, the captain's dinner. It was quiet on deck, and as the ship plowed silently through the waters, I felt like I was the only one on board. It seemed the perfect moment to throw a (respectful) challenge to the Lord. "Okay, Lord," I wrote, "we're going into my tenth ministry year in the same city. What do you have for me?"

I posed the question and kept writing. It was very quiet. The late afternoon sun was hot on my face; the air was salty and fresh. I felt energized and ready to take on the next big thing in life. So, I started to scribble out, freestyle, some of my goals, my hopes, and even some far-out wishes. Whatever came to me at the moment, I wrote it down—I knew the Lord would help me sort it out later. Well, this is funny. One of the phrases I wrote down included a word I don't even use: *"Engross yourself in the soccer team."*

Huh? Now, I love sports. I think I was born with a basketball in my hands. I've been a player and a coach, and I've played on more teams and in more pick-up games than I can count. Basketball is in my bones. But soccer? It's not one of the sports I follow.

I stared at the words I had written in my journal. To think of soccer was unusual; to use the word *engross* was, well ... a little weird. I never use that word. But there it was. I remember squinting out at sea, trying to figure out what that odd sentence meant. Those of us who are dedicated to mentoring young people in high school, and we know that when somebody says, "See you at the game," they mean basketball or football. (At least they did in 1994.) I had never gone to a soccer game, and I didn't even know where they played. So, I was really thrown off to see those words on the page. But at the same time, I knew they meant something, and that they were clearly from the Lord.

So, as soon as I got home from the cruise, I looked up the name of the varsity soccer coach and gave him a call. I explained I was from Young Life and was to build friendships with many of the high school kids who played sports. "I just want you to know you're going to see me around," I said, "I won't stay very long, but I'm going to come to your practices and your games. You don't have to tell anybody who I am; I just want you to know that if you ever need anything, let me know. I want to help."

The soccer coach was a believer, and although we never met, he knew of me and my work with Young Life. He made it clear that my call meant a lot to him. "That would be great if you could come around!" he said.

So, I began to hang around the soccer field. I was the quiet, tall guy who stood behind the coach and his small band of assistants. I found that it didn't take long to be drawn into the soccer experience, either. About forty kids were turning up for the "daily double" practices that were in August—twenty kids on the junior varsity team and twenty on the varsity.

Thing was, I *still* didn't know why the Lord had sent me to the soccer field. In the meantime, I was looking for ways to be useful, and it occurred to me—this was August, and hotter than Hades—"I bet these guys would appreciate cold drinks." So, one day, I bought coolers of Snapples. It was like I had turned loose an army. I watch forty and more kids tearing toward me as if a general had yelled, "Charge!" So, I was the happy Snapple distributor, passing out bottles and chatting with the kids as they grabbed an "icy-cold" before heading back to the field.

Except for one kid. I noticed him out of the corner of my eye; he was all alone in the nearby baseball dugout, messing with his cleats or something. He didn't even seem connected to the soccer practice. Since it was "hotter 'n blazes," I figured he could use a cold drink, too. So, scooping up two bottles (one for him and one for me, in case he wanted to talk), I loped over to the dugout and said, "Hey, I noticed you didn't get one. Here you go ..."

"I don't want your f----ng Snapple!" the kid shouted at me. I was shocked but managed to say with relative calm, "Oh, come on, you've got to be thirsty ..."

"Leave me alone!" Something more was going on, but at the moment, all I could think was that the kid thought if he took the Snapple, that meant I was trying to lure him into Young Life. Of course, I didn't mean that, so I set the bottle on the bench and left.

That was my first big hint that the Lord was in the process of answering my question on the cruise ship, "What do you have for me?" He had sent me to a soccer field to point out a young man who clearly was hurting.

A little later, the Lord showed me another reason why He needed me—needed someone!—to *engross yourself in the soccer team.*

One afternoon, I arrived at practice and immediately sensed tension buzzing through the whole team. Sure enough, the news was terrible. That morning, the mother of one of their teammates was found murdered. Actually, I was better prepared than I would have been because I had gotten a call earlier that day from a colleague who had heard the news from kids in his own Young Life ministry.

I said to my colleague, "Give me everything you know."

Dominic was a varsity soccer player and the victim's son. He was from a single-parent home and lived alone with his mom. He was always a good kid and was on the honor roll. He told the cops that his mom went for a walk the night before and never came back, and the next morning, he got up and went to school. (Well, there's a red flag—who just gets up in the morning and finds his mom missing, doesn't tell anybody, and just heads off for school?)

With a sigh, I told my colleague, "I think Dominic did it." Three months later, everything came out. Yes, Dominic murdered his mother. He stabbed her thirty-one times. The shock waves that went through the school, and even worse, directly through the heart of the soccer team, are indescribable. These are young teens—sophomores, juniors, in high school—and they had to come to grips with the fact that their friend and teammate had killed his mother.

There's no doubt that the Lord wanted to be with Dominic and all these kids at this disturbing time. Do you know why I know that? First of all, in the four weeks after the tragedy, nearly all forty kids on that soccer team ended up coming to Young Life. We were able to care for and support nearly all of them and hold them up in prayer and support—and a lot of food! I'm in awe of how the Lord arranged for me to be there, and long before I understood why. He needed somebody to open the door to Young Life. He knew every kid on that team would be needing His help, and they needed a pathway to get there.

And Dominic needed help most of all. Dominic didn't have a dad at his side, and I was privileged to be there to help him navigate through this catastrophe of his own making. I was one of two people, besides his lawyer, who could sit with him before the court proceedings. His sentence was to serve time in juvenile detention until he was twenty-one years old. The Lord knew Dominic would need someone to help him through this terrible trauma. Yes, he was guilty, but it turned out that childhood abuse had filled him with explosive rage. I was in awe and humbled that the Lord had arranged for me to be there to help him and pray for him.

Then, the Lord revealed even more. Remember the kid who rejected the cold Snapple with some colorful language? His name was Sabo, and he was one of the kids drawn to Young Life during that troubling fall when the murder happened. He'd come to the dinners we held before the Young Life meetings, but after he ate, and just before the meeting started, he'd ask me, "Okay, so when does the meeting end?" "Nine o'clock," I'd say. "Okay, I'll be back then," Sabo said, and he'd disappear.

I got very fond of the angry Sabo. At dinner, he talked about the challenges he faced and what troubled him, but he just wasn't ready to make a commitment to the Lord by coming to Young Life.

Until some weeks later, when Sabo accepted Christ as his Lord and Savior.

I still don't know why I wrote *"engross yourself in the soccer team"* on that cruise ship from Bermuda, but the Lord sure got His point across! So many kids on the soccer team met the Lord that year. On the wall of my office right now is a jersey with all their signatures on it because they wanted to show how thankful they were to get through an astonishing year that included both a murder and meeting the Lord. Although I had never been to a soccer practice or a soccer game, the Lord needed somebody on that soccer field to help Him, and I was available.

All I can say is, when you challenge the Lord, "What do You have for me?" be ready to follow through because He'll let you know.

For proof that the Lord is always sizing up our availability and directing our steps, I often think about this: Dominic was arrested at school. After school that day, all the soccer kids showed up at my house. A few weeks before, they didn't even know I existed. But that night, they were in shock, moving in slow motion. They needed a place to be safe and to pray. They didn't know where else to go or what else to do.

But the Lord knew.

FLIGHT PLANS

When you pray, do you ever get an unexpected inspiration to do something, visit someone, or make a personal change in your life?

Think of one of those inspirations—what did you do with it?

What was the outcome?

Have you ever rejected an inspiration in prayer and wished you had a "do-over?" How could you correct it now?

Can you think of someone right now who is hurting, sad, or in trouble that you could pray for or reach out to?

THE DEAD VAN

Sometimes, God answers crazy prayers just to show us He can. I learned that truth one Friday night when a small miracle met us in the middle of nowhere.

That weekend, we had gathered for a weekend camp at Breakaway Lodge, a popular Young Life camp. I was an assistant coach. Now, the team is made up of good kids and fine athletes, but it's also true they are all on a journey to figure out how to live as good young men, and the process isn't easy. Some kids have trouble conforming to a group; some are even a little rebellious. We roll with it; we know it's tough for teenagers. That weekend, I sensed that one of the more restless kids might need extra psyching up to get involved with the faith and prayer questions of the next few days. So, after dinner, I invited Chad, a very smart kid who questioned everything, to join me at a weekend camp with Young Life at Breakaway Lodge, with the stipulation that, on Saturday, we would leave camp to attend the Varsity basketball playoff game an hour away in Portland, Oregon. We left camp Saturday night at about five o'clock. We made it to Portland and enjoyed the game. About ten that night, we left the arena and started back for camp, but not before stopping for snacks. Then we hit the road. By that time, it was almost midnight.

Our drive was about an hour and a half along a two-lane road called the Van Duzer Corridor. By day, it's a stunning highway that curves through towering pines and dense forestland. By night, it's like driving through a long, black tunnel.

As we cruised toward home, I figured there was no better time to keep Chad focused on the weekend. Sure, it's a basketball weekend, but the mission of Young Life is to introduce young people to Jesus Christ and help them grow in their faith. We do that through sports and fun and adventurous experiences (like basketball) because the best way to motivate kids is when they are happy and absorbed in wholesome activities. Anyway, the role of the speaker (that's me) is to share in charge of the "why" of the weekend—why Jesus? So, I give a series of talks. Friday's talk asks the question, "Who is God?" On Saturday morning, the kids learn why Jesus died on the cross. It's structured so that by Sunday morning, each young person has the knowledge and opportunity, if they feel ready, to accept Jesus as their Lord and Savior.

But it's the Saturday night talk that's the most powerful. And now, on this dark, desolate, and deserted road, I figure it's the perfect setting to tell Chad about it. It's my most personal talk of all because it touches on the dark, desolate, and deserted place inside each of us.

"So, tell me, are you completely, one hundred percent happy?" In the dark, I can hear Chad grunt and chuckle. Clearly, the answer is "no"—hardly surprising! I begin to talk about the hole that exists in every person's heart (and teenagers can feel especially lost). We can spend an entire lifetime trying to fill it up with stuff that doesn't matter or that hurts us. All the stuff that keeps us from finding real happiness. I tell Chad that the unfilled empty place in his heart can only be filled by one thing, and it's not partying or drinking or girls. It's by forming a relationship with Jesus Christ.

Silence in the van. I know he's thinking this through because it's a message that kids can relate to, especially on a weekend. The world tells kids that if they just party some more, maybe do drugs, or try to mess around with girls, they'll make that hollow thing in their hearts go away. Instead, the loneliness only gets worse.

"If you just give ..."

I don't have a chance to finish my sentence. We hear a couple of clicks, a grinding sound, and the van wheezes to a complete stop. It's like life had been sucked right out from under us. Before it goes completely dead, I manage to steer us onto the side of the road. Right away, I feel myself shifting to high alert. This 15-year-old kid is my responsibility, and we're sitting in pitch blackness on a two-lane road about forty miles from help. This was before people carried cellphones, and there was no way to reach the outside world.

Well, Sco, it's time to figure something out.

So, I get out and open the hood. If the whole situation didn't feel so serious, I would have burst out laughing. Hey, I don't know anything about cars! Zero. I don't even know how to change the oil in my *own* car. Helplessly, I survey the hunk of machinery before me. We're in pitch darkness, and all I see is a shadowy mess of tubes and hoses connected to a big engine block. Now what?

Then something even worse happens. Chad wants to know what I'm going to do. "Do you know how to fix it?" Chad has left the van and is peering with me into the dark hole of tubes and hoses. He's a question-everything kind of kid, but I sense he's a little scared right now but won't admit it. I also sense he completely trusts what I'm going to do. (Little does he know I haven't a clue.) So, I decide honesty is best. "I don't know yet," I say. "Let's get back in the van while I figure this out."

In the dark and cold (it's only early spring), I'm aware of the ninth grader beside me and that his anxiety is rising, too. I try the ignition. Nothing.

"Let's just wait a few minutes and try again." In fact, we sit there for almost half an hour. All the while, my mind is racing, trying to think of the next thing to do. We make small talk (we're too edgy to concentrate on anything deep), and I ask Chad what class he likes the most, what's the hardest thing to learn about basketball—anything to keep him from worrying that we're on a deserted road in the middle of nowhere.

I get out one more time, open the hood, wiggle some wires. Get back in, turn the key. Nothing. I say a silent prayer, *"Okay, Lord, it's time to go all or nothing."*

"Okay," I announce, "We're not getting anywhere with this van, but that doesn't mean there's nothing we can do. We can come to the Lord and ask for His help *right now.* What I mean is, it's time to put the Lord to the test."

There's a moment of silence, and then Chad starts stammering out uneasy questions like, "What does *that* mean?" So I plunge forward—"Have you ever tried praying out loud?"

Chad pipes up right away. "I've never prayed *at all*—and for sure, not out loud!" I can tell he's as embarrassed as a 15-year-old would be at the thought of praying. Worse, praying out loud! As for me, I'm pretty much at the end of my rope. In fact, I'm at the same place I was telling my passenger when the van conked out—that when everything else fails, when you're scared and don't know what to do next, Christ is the answer.

"If you just give ..."

"Listen, if we just give Him a chance, Christ can help us!" (I have Chad's attention. Okay, that's a start.) "Remember what we were talking about? It's only when you come to the end of yourself, to the end of your rope, that you realize, okay, who can help me? The Bible says that for us, it's impossible to help ourselves, but for God, *nothing* is impossible. Well, right now, guys, we have needs. We've got to get home. I'm telling you that everything the Bible says is true, and because it's true, the time has come to put the Lord to the test, to ask Him to help us *right now."*

I knew Chad was weirded out by the thought of praying. His family were nonbelievers; he never went to church. But there, in the cold and dark, I watch Chad step into another kind of darkness—the dark that comes right before faith breaks through. With a sigh and some self-conscious grumbling, Chad says, "Okay, if You're up there, can you fix this van?" There's a moment of silence, and then I hear a muffled, self-conscious chuckle, and Chad bursts out, "I don't know what You're doing up there or even if You *can* do anything, but we could use some help down here!"

For a non-praying kid, Chad's prayer was open and pretty special. For sure, I could appreciate that it was probably tough to say out loud! After a pause, I pitched in. "Lord, we don't know what to do. We have run out of our options. I don't know anything about engines. No one's driving by. We want to get back. We want to get in our *uncomfortable* bunk beds with our sleeping bags!" (At that, we both snorted a weak chuckle. Uncomfortable bunk beds sounded pretty good about then.)

With every ounce of faith I had—and at that point, I wasn't sure it was much—I burst out with, "Lord, we believe that You can start this engine if You want to. So, we're putting our trust in You right now, that You're going to start this engine, as crazy as this sounds."

Guess God hears crazy.

I turn the key, and the engine rumbles to life. We sit there, stunned. (Hey, even if you have faith, it's okay to be amazed by a miracle!) By the sounds we heard when the van died, something had broken inside the engine. It wasn't a battery thing. There's no way it could have "repaired" itself, but it did. God had answered our prayers—*Chad's* prayers—and was showing His authority over our world. He was showing this skeptical kid that He was really there.

We allow ourselves a round of cheering, and then Chad announces, "Well, if that's what the Lord can do, I want Him in my life."

And you know what? Chad followed through. That weekend, Chad stood up and publicly and bravely proclaimed his faith in the Lord.

It wasn't a one-weekend thing, either. It's more than thirty-four years later now, and Chad and I are good friends. He's become a fine man. What's more, he helped his mom, dad, and brother (all of them nonbelievers!) meet the Lord. And who knows how many others?

All I know is so many lives were changed on that desolate stretch of road, and it all hinged on the moment when the engine started. I have no idea why it started, except the Lord answered our prayers. But what I find kind of shocking is that, even after the engine started, you second-guess yourself. *The van overheated. That "broke" sound didn't happen. It would have started anyway.* That kind of thing. Even when something good happens, maybe there's a human reaction to justify a miracle. Maybe the kid with the five loaves and two fish went around saying, "It wasn't all me; somebody else must've brought more."

Maybe that would be true if prayer changed things only once or twice. But if you give God a chance, it happens over and over again! In this case, it happened on a deserted road with a scared kid (and a scared driver) in a van that clearly clunked out. Prayer works, and sometimes in the oddest ways and circumstances. In this case, prayer was the ultimate mechanic.

FLIGHT PLANS

Have you ever been at the end of your rope and prayed a crazy prayer? What happened?

Sometimes, we all feel a prayer hasn't been answered—but *something* happened: What was it? Maybe you lost the job you prayed for but found something else? Or the dream house you hoped to buy didn't work out? Whatever it was, can you see a greater good in what happened instead?

Do you resist saying crazy prayers because you don't believe God hears them? What if you challenged yourself to try? Think of something crazy that's deep in your heart that you really want, but you think there's no hope. Now, pray for it!

Now, give God time to act—write down a date here _____.
Make it long enough away to make sense (if your prayer is to find the right person to marry and you haven't met them yet, you really need to give God six months, or maybe even a year!) But if you are out of work and have only enough money for one more mortgage payment, challenge God to turn your desperate circumstances around quickly.)

HOUSE FOR SALE (FOREVER)

You know those times when your mind and stomach are churning with worry? Talk about the need to get going on a crazy prayer!

Years ago, we had a phrase to describe life's heaviest worries: *the stuff that weighs down your backpack.* That's what we called it, anyway, during our breakfasts at the Original Pancake House.

At the time I'm talking about, I was twenty-six years old and the area director for Young Life in Salem, Oregon. Three days a week, at 6:30 a.m. sharp, I would meet the sophomore boys for breakfast at the Original Pancake House. Over pancakes and waffles, we'd eat, laugh, and shoot questions back and forth about life. It was open season on everything—God, girls, grades, sports—whatever was on their minds that day. We talked about all the highs and lows they were going through, and we'd relate them to the Bible, and how God uses those circumstances to make us better people, and how He can intervene in those circumstances to help us.

Anyway, on one particular day, I was pretty distracted because I had a lot weighing down *my* backpack. In fact, I was pretty low. I had gotten myself into financial trouble, and I didn't know what to do about it.

A few years earlier, I had bought my first house. The house was twenty-three years old, nine hundred square feet, and it cost me $40,000. Just right for a single guy starting out. By the time I was twenty-six, the real estate market had taken off, and my little starter house was now valued at $70,000. It felt like a windfall, and it made me feel giddy, especially when I caught sight of a much better house and realized, yeah, I could swing it. The new house was going for $92,000, and it was 1,600 square feet and had three bedrooms. But I had to jump on it, you know?

My dad tried to bring me back down to earth. "Eric, it's your house; you can do what you want, but I would not buy *that* house until you sell *your* house. That's my advice."

I listened, and I pondered (for about ninety seconds), and then I told myself, "This new house is gonna be snapped up quick. I have to jump on it." So, I bought the new house and put my starter house on the market.

Honestly, I should have listened to my dad. Especially since he rarely gave unsolicited advice, his words should have blared in my head like an emergency siren. Sure enough, six months later, I was deep under water. My starter house was truly qualifying as a *non-starter*—it hadn't budged off the market. Not one offer.

So, by the time I got to the Original Pancake House that particular day, my insides were in serious turmoil. Two mortgage payments were due in a few days, and I was tapped out. As we sat there over our pancakes and waffles, I tried to stuff my problem away in my brain and think about what was really important here. "It's not about me," I reminded myself, "it's about these young men! C'mon, Sco, focus!"

The breakfast was winding down, and we had gone around the table while each kid identified his backpack that day: "What's weighing down your backpack? Or, what's making your backpack lighter today?"

We had one kid to go. I didn't want to show it, but I was nervous, jumpy and wanted to be alone to gnash over my problem. I stole a look at my watch. *(It's 7:40. Almost time to wrap this up, guys.)* The last kid was Paul Richter, a good kid, but that day, he was late for breakfast. His hair was damp, and his letterman's jacket was falling off one shoulder.

I asked the question, just like I had with the other guys. "Okay, Paul, what's in your backpack today?"

I'll never forget what happened next. Paul kind of cleared his throat and said, "Scofield, do you realize you've never answered that question yourself? How do you get out of here every week without answering the question about *your* backpack?"

"Nah, I'm not gonna answer the question," I said, laughing it off. But the guys must have sensed something because suddenly, they were all piling on me. "We're not leaving until you answer the question! What's in *your* backpack, Scofield?"

In an instant, it was like all my worries and fears were flooding together in my mind, and I had to find a way to release them. "Okay, okay," I said, "I'll answer your question. To tell you the truth, my backpack is heavy right now. I know you guys probably don't understand a mortgage or how serious it is to miss a monthly payment, but I did something dumb. My dad told me not to do it, but I did it. I bought a new house before I sold the one I have. Now, I'm paying off two mortgages, and I can't swing it anymore. Two payments are coming up. To tell you the truth, guys, I don't know what to do."

Paul, his hair and jacket all sideways, looked at me thoughtfully, and then he made an announcement: "Scofield, we're gonna pray right now. Everybody get up. C'mon, arm in arm!" Right there in the Original Pancake House, we all stood up and linked arms, and Paul began to pray. "Lord," he said, "we love Sco, and his backpack is heavy, so we're going to ask that You sell his house. You sell his house *today*. That's what we're asking, and we believe You will do it." Paul looked around the group. "Do you guys agree?" ("Yeah, yeah, yeah!") "Alright, there you go, and AMEN."

I remember thinking to myself, "Oh, that's so cute." I told the guys, "Thank you so much!" but inside, I was thinking, "That's not how it works ..."

So, I went on with my day and didn't think anything more about it until I got home at about four o'clock and the phone rang. It was my real estate agent, Nancy Fiskum, and she was kind of chuckling. "Well, you must have done something good today! You haven't one offer—you have *two*. Both came in the last twenty-five minutes, and one of them is cash. No contingencies."

I stammered out something about the young men who had prayed over my heavy backpack that very morning, and Nancy said, "Well, the Lord has sure answered your prayer! You better get those boys together and tell them what happened." Of course, I did the very next week. (Here's the great thing about young people who aren't cynical about life—if you open the door to the Lord when they're young, you've given them the chance to build up a great faith. I saw that in action when I told the group because they stared at me like, yeah, so what else is new? "Well, sure, Scofield, we knew it would sell! We prayed, didn't we?")

This wasn't the end of my house-selling saga. It was as if the Lord wanted to show that He doesn't just answer a prayer; sometimes, He hits the answer right out of the ballpark.

First, here's the rest of *that* story: My non-starter house turned out to have the fastest close that Prudential had ever done in South Salem. No appraisals. Just boom, boom, boom. Sold. You'd think a guy would learn—*prayer works*. But sometimes, the Lord needs to do a lot of shoving and pushing to get that lesson into our brains (into my brain, anyway).

Life goes on. About five years later, Marni and I were married, we had our first baby, and I took a new role for Young Life in Houston, Texas. Now, it wasn't like I was an executive for some big corporation like Amazon or Apple, where they take care of selling your house, and might even buy it from you if it doesn't sell. No, I was all on my own.

You'd think I'd learn. But once again, anxiety was tickling me; I didn't like having an unsold house hanging over my head! For sure, it was on my mind, and at one of my Tuesday Bible studies, I told the group about the first story and linked it to the incredible, crazy power of prayer. This time, our setting was the party room at a local McDonald's, and the crowd included a passionate sophomore football quarterback, A.J. Parnell. When I told the group I was gonna be pouring a lot of prayer into selling this second house, A.J. pipes up:

"Scofield, you know we can do the same thing right now, don't you? C'mon, everybody, stand up! We're gonna pray."

I'm telling you, it was like A.J. Parnell was Paul Richter incarnate from the Pancake House! Once again, when least expected (and when I was once again carrying a heavy backpack), a young guy stood up and courageously called everybody to prayer.

This was seven o'clock in the morning. No more than three hours later, I got a phone call from my real estate agent, who announced, "We just got a full price offer on your house!"

Now, you can't make this stuff up. At least you can't make it up to be *believable* unless it really happened, and it did. This time, I wasn't in desperate financial straits, but selling the house was still a factor in my life. It was just as if the Lord was saying, "Listen, I'm *always* here to help you. It doesn't matter whether you're in the most desperate circumstances of your life or the most ordinary. I won't always give you what you want because it might not be good for you. I won't always answer you right away, either, because my timing is better than yours. But I *will* answer you, and sometimes, like with your houses, I'll do it right away, *just because I can.*"

I learned so much from my house capers. The major one: Never discount the awesome effects of praying with others: *"Wherever two or more are gathered in my name, there am I in the midst of them."* (Matthew 18:20) and John 15:7: *"Remain in me and I in you, and ask anything you wish, and it will be given to you."*

So, if you're facing something that seems insurmountable and unchangeable, gather good people around you and start to pray. If you're alone, that's okay, too. And when you're worried, stressed, and terrified, try a crazy prayer! I've come to believe that God really loves crazy prayers. Why? Because those are the prayers where only He can help, and He *wants* to help. Those are the prayers we can *never, ever* answer ourselves.

FLIGHT PLANS

Okay, no more fooling around! You've read enough stories now about real-life crazy prayers that are answered. Time to step up and pray a crazy prayer of your own! What might be a few crazy prayers you might have?

MIRACLE SONS

Marni and I were married on August 28, 1999. We joked how much we were looking forward to spending the next millennium together. Like every couple, we had to merge our boundaries (we both agreed that a household budget was a must), and we shared most of the same expectations. (Did Marni mind that I might be transferred a lot in my job? No, she was good with that.)

There was one expectation that we had to put gently aside, at least at first. We weren't sure we could have kids. For years, Marni had endured endometriosis, a painful condition that makes pregnancy problematic, and she had been taking birth control pills, which are commonly prescribed to relieve the pain. Put everything together, and doctors told her she was an unlikely candidate for motherhood. Okay. Thanks for telling us. We will deal with it.

Well, what we came to know is that God shows off His best work in the awesome, glorious reality of human life. When He's in action, all kinds of crazy prayers are on the table:

Around November 15, my bride handed me an early Christmas present—a tree ornament. It was a big red ceramic heart—probably a Pottery Barn gift. We have it to this day, and it always takes a very strong branch! We were going to have a baby! All of a sudden, we had to make a sharp pivot on what our life was going to be like—360 degrees. Even in the middle of the first shock, we were over-the-moon happy. Marni had a high-risk pregnancy and needed bed rest, so we moved forward carefully and prayed a lot, but nothing could take away our joy.

Minutes after our son, Hudson, was born, July 31, 2000, I was holding him in my arms when the doctor came over to me. In that even, unemotional way doctors have, he said, "Your son is a miracle." Then he explained that the placenta and umbilical cord were barely attached in three places. If they detached during pregnancy, the baby would have been stillborn. In effect, our boy had survived a hurricane on a life preserver that was attached to the boat by a thread! But I was only half listening as the doctor was explaining all this. I was too filled with joy to let anything else into my head. None of that bad stuff had happened. Our little guy was here, safe and sound.

We named our miracle son "Hudson" for a reason. He was named after Hudson Taylor, an amazing 18th-century Christian missionary from England who evangelized China. The connection meant a lot to us. Taylor had spent time studying to be a midwife, of all things, and by the time Hudson Scofield entered our life, we felt we had learned more than our share about how to bring a healthy child into the world.

Hudson grew fast and strong, and we hoped to gift him with a sibling. Instead, we learned that we should never try to figure out where God is going next because "His ways are not our ways" (Isaiah 55:8-9). We learned this mysterious truth because the joy of Hudson's birth was followed by five miscarriages. That was a hard time. Marni was suffering in a way that I, as a man, could only partly understand. We held on to each other.

That was hard. We'd go to Young Life camps, and most of the staff were couples, and it seemed (to us, anyway) they were 24/7 baby factories! It seemed every conversation started with "Yes, we're on our fourth …" or "Our fifth …." I'll be honest, we winced a little every time there was an update. By the same token, Hudson was closing in on his sixth birthday, and we were moving through his growing-up stages happily. We just wished he could enjoy growing up with a brother or sister. To be honest (and this is something that effortlessly fertile parents probably don't think about), it stings to hear all the cheerful talk about the most organic baby food and the latest hi-tech strollers. But after a while, I just kind of shook myself and said, "Honey, we're blessed. We have a great life. We have Hudson. Let's be thankful and not think about this anymore."

Well, I've learned never to underestimate Marni, and certainly not when we're faced with a high wall. I was ready to find another route to our family's happiness and move on, but Marni was determined to find a way *through* that wall. One day, she walked into the room and said, "What would you think of adoption?"

"Oh, gosh," I said, "It takes so much time. It costs a fortune. Can't we just be happy with one?" Marni was gentle about it, but she wouldn't give up, either. We went back and forth. We talked to people we trusted. One night, we were at the house of friends of ours, and they told us about a couple who had adopted a child, but not from an agency. Their baby came because they knew someone who knew someone, and the biological parents were amazing people—the epitome of goodness and kindness—practically saints, on and on and on.

That's when I made an announcement that has become a classic line in our family:

"Listen, we're not doing this. I'm happy for that family and their storybook ending. Good for them. But if you think the quarterback of the football team and the homecoming queen are gonna get pregnant and have a baby and deliver it to our doorstep, it's not gonna happen!"

That was in June. In August, I had relented enough to agree with Marni to start an agency adoption process, but it began in a weird and depressing way. Our goal was to find a child to love, and instead, we were in an office being told we had to swipe our Visa card first. Then we learned we would have to meet with the grandmother of our future child because the teenage parents were off doing drugs. No, this didn't feel right.

We backed off, but of course, we kept praying. What did God want for our life? Hudson rounded out our happiness completely, but did God have another child who belonged with us, but we just didn't know it yet?

One day in October that year, I had just wrapped up a speaking engagement at a Young Life banquet in Santa Barbara and was making the four-hour drive down the 101 back home to San Diego. I was admiring the gorgeous blue Pacific off to my right (that's how well I remember the exact moment) when my phone rang. I was surprised at the caller because it was a woman I knew only slightly. She was in Bible study with my mom.

"Your mom asked us to remember you and Marni in prayer because you're trying to decide about adopting," the woman said. "Well, a girl who runs our after-school program for kids has a 16-year-old brother. His girlfriend is pregnant. Would you like to hear more about it?"

I said sure, but then came the deal breaker—they lived three states away. The odds of figuring out those logistics with complete strangers—teenagers, yet!—were small to none.

"Would you at least ask Marni?" she said.

"No, I'm sorry, I can't do that," I said. "The distance, the age of the kids ... I think it would end up being a disappointment almost as sad as a miscarriage. I won't do that to Marni."

"Can I tell you at least something about these two young kids?"

"Okay, go ahead."

"Well," she said, "he's the quarterback of the football team, and she plays varsity soccer and was just on the homecoming court. They're really nice kids ...."

At that, my mind went into kind of a happy blur. It was as if God reached His hand in my car, smacked me on the side of my face, and said, "See? What have I always told you? Don't put restrictions on me!"

When I got home, I slammed together some photos with a hastily typed four-page family biography and sent it off to the caller. I still didn't tell Marni. I didn't want to crush her; I was flinching myself at the disappointment that still seemed inevitable.

But all I can say is when God acts, He acts. The 16-year-old father was given our family packet, and he took it to his mother. And his mother said, "*Sco?* This is from *Sco?*" Turns out she was a counselor at the camp where, for two years in a row, I had been the camp speaker! We knew each other. Even sight unseen, the boy and his family thought Marni and I sounded like the perfect fit.

Not so fast. The young mother and her parents put their foot down. Their daughter was seven and a half months pregnant, and the family was already involved with an adoption agency. Derail *that?* No way! The young father-to-be even pleaded with the agency people, "I think we've found the perfect family!"

Meanwhile, at our end, we're going along, thinking, "We have this. This is the answer to our prayers; this is our child!" I called the adoption agency myself and, with all innocence and eagerness, asked, "How do we get this rolling?" And they laughed at me. Have you participated in an official home study? ("Huh? What's that?") Are you enrolled in our system, and have you paid the required fee? ("Um, no ...") Do you know there's a waiting list and many parents ahead of you for this baby? ("Well, we assumed there's a waiting list, but what if we're the perfect family for this child?!") Sorry, you're not in our system. ("Okay, so how long will a home study take to get *into* your system?") Three months. *("Three months?!?")* By then, the baby would be over a month old. At every turn, we were slammed against a harsh and cold bureaucracy.

But the bureaucracy hadn't met the Scofields. I'm not an "8" on the Enneagram personality spectrum for nothing—"Active Controller" is my name. And Marni? I've already told you that she'll go through walls to solve a problem. She is a fighter. But most of all, *God was with us.* By then, we had the conviction that our prayers were in the process of being answered, and now God was asking us to do our part. So, we went to work.

(By the way, I'm telling you all this as I go along to prove that whatever your circumstances, if you have prayed for God's help and you have the conviction, He is with you; no matter how many setbacks, *you must never give up.)*

Okay, what about the home study? Marni got it done in five days: FBI checks, financial checks, family background checks, blood records, everything! Impossible, but she did. Then we called the agency back. "We are complying, we have the home study, and we want to be considered for this baby!" They grudgingly relented, telling us that now we need to meet the young couple and the girl's family in person. ("We're on our way!") We flew across those three states like it was across the street.

I won't kid you. The meeting with the two kids and the girl's family had its uncomfortable moments. (God may have every intention of answering your prayers, but that doesn't mean He wants it to be easy.) I work with teenagers every day. I love high school kids. But when I met the teenage birth parents-to-be for the first time, I felt like I had sprouted two left feet. Marni felt her heart was being tugged every which way, too; the significance of what we were doing was so profound. But no amount of awkwardness or discomfort could dampen our growing happiness—not even the inevitable swipe of the Visa card that made it official.

And you know what? Once the bureaucratic ordeal was over, everything was different. We merged into what we were meant to be all along—families bonding together, linked by the joy of a new child coming into the world. I asked the girl's family if we could take them out to dinner. "I know it feels like we've come through the back door, but I just want to hear your story, and I want to tell you our story. I do feel like God's in the mix here ..." The girl's parents said, "No, not a restaurant; come over to our house for dinner!"

The adoption agency workers might think *they* made it official; it was really our three families that did that. Somehow, each of us knew that we had to treat each other with respect and sensitivity for the deep and complicated feelings involved.

A little later, back in Oregon, we had an awesome dinner with the parents of the birth mother. Hudson, by then six years old, came with us that night, and Marni and I have an indelible memory of watching him play pinball on the floor that night, excited to know his little brother was on the way. For Hudson, it was like waiting for Christmas. For us, too. Magical.

On November 20, 2006, Charlie was born, and shortly after, he found his place in Marni's arms. We had a little ceremony for Jonny and Molly, giving each of them a special gift and thanking them as best we could for their gift to us. Our Charlie! Then, we piled into a Lincoln Continental that I rented and went on to celebrate an unforgettable day.

Since that joyous day, the two teenage birth parents have completed college and have gone on to marry other people and start their own families. We stay in touch on social media, and the birth mom and grandmother send Charlie a gift and a card every birthday and Christmas. He's a teenager now, and he has a photo of his birth mom in his room, right there where he can see it every day, just him and her, with some great memories of a birthday she attended one year.

As for us, Marni and I have our boys, Hudson and Charlie, our miracle sons. Each of them is proof that while some prayers may seem crazy, they can also be the most glorious prayers of all:

One son came to us attached to life by a thread.

The other son came to us (despite my pompous pronouncement that it would never happen) through the generosity of a quarterback and a prom queen.

God must be chuckling over that one.

FLIGHT PLANS

Think about your kids: What is special about each one? How would your life be different if he or she wasn't there?

What would be your "big impossible miracle" that you are not so sure you want to add to the list of hopes and prayers?

WHEN ANGELS TAKE COMMAND

Father Rock was an elderly man in his late eighties when Marni and I went to visit him for what we thought could be the last time. But even before we got there, the Lord was preparing a moment that would blast away the usual meaning of *"last time."* And the Lord did it in the space of a few seconds.

Thinking back on it, *of course* this amazing event happened! We were on our way to visit an amazing man, the one-of-a-kind Father Rock.

Father Rock was (and still is!) one of those people you can't wait to see again. It's kind of funny to think how many, many people care about him because for twenty-six years, he was a monk who lived a completely solitary life on the (appropriately named) Mount Angel, Oregon. All that time, he rarely spoke with another human being; he spent his life talking with God.

But clearly, God wanted more people besides Himself to enjoy Father Rock. After a quarter-century alone, this wonderful monk heard God calling him to change everything. He left the solitary life to become a "working" priest, who went out into the world to gather people around him, people who need God in their lives. But God wasn't done yet. He had another invitation for Father Rock, and it came when he was about sixty-five and was disguised in a case of deadly prostate cancer. That's what made Father Rock decide to retire—but not from life.

After he recovered, he scraped together the few pennies he had to his name and built a home just outside of Scappoose, Oregon. But he built the home not for himself; he opened it to all his friends for retreats and times of prayerful reflection. But leave it to Father Rock to prove that God, prayer, and celebration can go together. He loved expressing his one-hundred-percent Italian heritage with booming welcomes, massive bear hugs, and amazing pasta dinners.

For years, I've been bringing kids and colleagues to meet Father Rock at his one-of-a-kind cabin on Fishhawk Lake. Father Rock called his home Rock Haven, and like everything else in his life, he made Rock Haven unique and unexpected. For example, he built his house backward so that the front door faces the sweet spot— a glittering lake tucked in a forest of pines. Everything about the house reflected Father Rock's personality. He wanted it to be simple yet genuine. He even made the curtains! But although he was sur-rounded by beauty, Father Rock didn't want people to forget life's ultimate goal. So, he added the "stations of the cross" on his property as a reminder of Christ's walk to Calvary, where He paid the ultimate price for our salvation.

Every time I was at Father Rock's, I would "hear God" in a fresh new way. I always thought of "Rocks," as I called him, as a modern-day Brother Lawrence—the saintly 17th-century monk who taught people to bring God into the ordinary circumstances of their lives. Anyway, it had been a long time since I had been to Rock Haven, and Marni had never been there. Hudson was about fifteen months old at the time, and I wanted both of them to meet this very special guy at Fishhawk Lake.

The thing is, it's a trek to get there. Fishhawk Lake is in a secretive place—it's encircled by thick pine forests, so you don't see the lake until you're almost upon it. For the last few miles, you're on a tight, curving road that demands all your attention. It's not a trip for white-knuckle drivers because chances are by the time you get there, you'll be a white knuckler, anyway.

Given everything that Father Rock and his Rock Haven have meant to me over the years, it was fitting that Marni and I were headed there when *it* happened.

That day, Marni and I left Seattle late. Traffic was terrible. Hudson was tucked down in his baby seat. It was one of those typical December days in the Pacific Northwest—rainy, windy, and gloomy. Leaves were flying everywhere and slicking up the roads. Not the best day for a jaunt. Usually, the drive to Fishhawk Lake is about three hours down I-5, but we knew we were going to miss our 6 o'clock pasta dinner with Father Rock by several hours.

It was about eight o'clock by the time we turned onto the curvy two-lane road that leads to Fishhawk Lake. The road is steep, with cliffs on one side, so we didn't talk much because we were concentrating so hard on the slick and shiny few inches of roadway that we could see in our high beams. But even though we were tired and stressed, we were getting excited, too—we were less than thirty minutes from Father Rock's hearty welcome and a big platter of Italian pasta.

Suddenly, just ahead of us, we were blinded by the lights of a huge log truck that had just come around a curve. Log trucks are everywhere in Oregon. They are massive, lumbering giants, and you don't mess with them anywhere.

At this moment, we had no choice. This log truck was one hundred percent in our lane and headed straight for us. To the right was nothing but a cliff.

In a lightning flash, I thought of Marni, our little Hudson in the back seat, how much I loved them, and the fact that our lives were over. No, we would never see Father Rock that night, or ever again. Our plans and dreams for the future were no more substantial than the rain on our windshield. God had other plans for us. We were seconds from eternity.

Wrapped in the dread and sorrow of that lightning flash going through my mind was a prayer to God to be with us.

Then, something *else* happened. I don't know any other way to describe this: Have you ever been on the "Pirates of the Caribbean" ride at Disneyland? As your boat heads up the hill of water to start the ride, there is a movie with a Pirate being shown on a vapor of steam. "Riders beware," he says, and as riders pass through, most wave their hands through the vapor screen.

The next thing I remember is a loud rushing wind and a sense of strong vapor running through our Jeep Cherokee.

The log truck became vapor, and it went right through our car. One moment, our car was filled with the headlights of a log truck that was about to smash into us. The next moment, the log truck had vaporized into nothing, and we were on the other side. We were all alone on a narrow, rainy road. The log truck headlights that filled our windshield? Vanished.

I managed to edge us over to the side of the road safely and stopped the car. My whole body was shaking. Next to me, Marni grabbed my hand, and we just sat there trembling and trying to breathe.

"Marni, what just happened?"

"I don't know."

We went over it at least four times, trying to make sense of it. That truck was inches from us—we both saw it. Now, it had vaporized and vanished in a single moment of—*what*?

When we got to Father Rock's house, we were still white-faced and trembling. He met us at the door, and immediately, his wide, welcoming smile vanished into a look of concern. Even before I had properly introduced Marni and Hudson to him, I couldn't do anything but burst out, "Rock, you're not gonna believe this!"

As I told the story of our near disaster, I saw the smile slowly come back to Father Rock's face. By the time I finished, his smile was an outright grin.

"Well, of course!" he said. "Don't you know the Lord can just do anything at any time? Psalm 91 says that *God commands His angels concerning you*. In His great love for you, the Lord chose a log truck and a two-lane road to make that psalm come alive, just for you. It's a great blessing! Now, how about dinner?"

All the times I've visited my good friend, Father Rock, I never learned a lesson like that. God used our visit to this amazing man to teach us something unforgettable about life. Our time on earth wasn't done. It didn't matter that a log truck was on the road that night, or that maybe the driver was sleepy, or maybe he was worried and inattentive, or maybe he couldn't see our tiny car through the rain. He was there, and we were there. But God had more plans for us on this earth, and so He made things *right*. He used his angels to protect us from that log truck.

If Marni wasn't there, I would not have believed it, and if I wasn't there, Marni would not have believed it. We don't know why He did it, or even *how* He did it, but the fact He *did* it at all—that is what's important! And it's shocking because it shows that angels are all around us, and God can command them to redirect even huge mistakes that are just about to happen.

What do you do with that? We don't give God the credit for being there. Some people will say, "Really? The Lord can work like *that* in my life?"

The answer is yes. As Father Rock might say, "You've got to stay connected to the Person, the God, who created you. He has put angels beside you. And He's always right there, ready to help!"

And sometimes, He helps before you even have time to ask.

FLIGHT PLANS

You've heard the stories. Crazy prayer is real, and God hears those prayers! What are you going to do about it? You know there are unanswered prayers in your own life, but you've never willed yourself to pray for them constantly and intentionally.

Time to do it!

APPENDIX
COVENANT WEEKEND MATERIALS

Resources included:

- Covenant Weekend
- Significant other Survey for Covenant Weekend
- Kid Survey for Covenant Weekend
- Spouse Survey for Covenant Weekend
- Friend / Parent Survey

COVENANT WEEKEND

[Date)

A man of many companions may come to ruin, but there is a Friend who sticks closer than a brother. Proverbs 1 8:24

Brothers,

I hope that you are looking forward to our annual gathering in Sunriver. This year promises to be yet another great time of sharing our stories and celebrating our God-givenrelationships with one another. Herb and Hanson are up to bat as coordinators and we are excited to take our turn.

Please use the following to assist you in capturing your life and sharing it with us.

The schedule begins with dinner (6pm) Saturday at the Lorenz's Sunriver cabin (directions to follow). Will this finally be the year that all of us arrive on time? More details about what to bring later.

FOOD FOR THOUGHT
STATEMENTS MADE BY MEN ON THEIR DEATHBED

- Even in the valley of the shadow of death, two and two do not make six (Tolstoy)
- How were the receipts today in Madison Square Garden? (PT Barnum)
- All of the wisdom of this world is but a tiny raft upon which we must set sail when we leave this earth. If only there was a firmer foundation upon which to sail, perhaps some divine word. (Socrates)
- I am about to take my last voyage, a great leap in the dark. (Thomas Hobbes)
- A lifelong agnostic, W.C. Fields was discovered reading a Bible on his deathbed. "I'm looking for a loophole," he explained.
- The meager satisfaction that man can extract from reality leaves him starving. (Sigmund Freud)

YOU HAVE 3 THINGS TO DO IN PREPARATION

1. ONE YEAR TIMELINE

- In addition to a list of events and special memories, identify the times of spiritual highs and lows for last year.
- Bring one selection from your journal to read to the group that illustrates one mark on your timeline.
- Reminder. The timeline is to note times, activities, and events that have impacted you greatly. These can be positive or negative events. For those events, identify how God is using those events to teach you about Himself and about yourself.

2. SPOUSE / FRIEND AND KID/FRIEND SURVEY

Here are the fundamentals:

1. Get the surveys to them ASAP so they have time to complete them.

2. Make sure you take them with you.

3. SELF SURVEY

The following are some questions that can help guide your thoughts and reflections. For each answer, I am asking myself to explain my answer.

As A Man

- Am I being a good steward of the body God gave me?
- Am I nurturing my most important relationships?
- Am I stewarding my finances in a way honoring to the Lord?
- Am I using my time wisely in pursuit of my particular purpose?
- Are my values reflected in the way I behave? Temptations, Struggles?

As a Christian

- Am I experiencing enough worship of my God?
- Am I more of a disciple of Jesus Christ than I was last year?
- Am I more of a servant of others, the church, my family than last year?
- Am I brining Christ into the center of my marriage, how, what?
- Am I experiencing true community with other Christians on a regular basis?

School Name
Street Address, City, St Zip Code
Phone: (585) 555-0125 | Web Site Address

Covenant Weekend November [Date]
Significant other Survey for Covenant Weekend. Year_____

Thank you for being a part of this special retreat this year. Please take some time and share your thoughts to the following questions. Be sure to give this to your 'man' as soon as possible. (at least a week before the retreat)

[Name]

1. If someone were to ask you, "Describe your current relationship." What would you say and why?

_____

_____

_____

2. What have been the biggest changes you have seen in Matt's life over the last year?

_____

_____

_____

3. What are you most proud of about Matt and what are you most excited about?

_____

_____

_____

4. What are the top three things Matt has done "right" or done "well" this past year?.

_____

_____

_____

5. What have been some of your thoughts about the health of your relationship?

_____

_____

_____

6. What are 3 romantic dates you would enjoy in 2007?

_____

_____

_____

7. What changes are you trying to make about yourself this next year and how can Matt help you?

_____

_____

_____

Covenant Weekend November [Date]

Kid Survey for Covenant Weekend. Year_____

Dear Son/Daughter, (*Mom's you will need to help*)
Your dad is going to spend a weekend with some of his friends that he has been hangin' out with for many years. It is a time of fun, friendship, and reflection. Your answers to the following questions are going to be very helpful. Thanks!

[name]

1. What have been some of the best times you have had with your dad this past year?

_____

_____

_____

_____

_____

_____

_____

_____

_____

_____

2. What are the best things about your dad?

_____

_____

_____

_____

_____

_____

_____

_____

3. If you had to give him some advice on being a better dad, what would it be and why?

_____

_____

_____

_____

_____

_____

_____

4. What are some things that you would like to talk with your dad about and why?

_____

_____

_____

_____

_____

_____

_____

_____

5. What are three things about your dad that he is really good at?

_____

_____

_____

_____

_____

_____

_____

_____

6. What are some of your fears that you would like your dad to pray for you about?

_____

_____

_____

_____

_____

_____

_____

_____

7. What is something really cool that you would like to do with your dad? What about a trip?

_____

_____

_____

_____

_____

_____

_____

Put your answers in a sealed envelope

Covenant Weekend November [Date]

Spouse Survey for Covenant Weekend. Year_____

Dear Spouse,

Thank you for being a part of this special retreat the last four years. Please take some time and share your thoughts to the following questions. Be sure to give this to your spouse as soon as possible. (at least a week before the retreat)

[Name]

1. If someone were to ask you, "Describe your current marriage relationship." What would you say and why?

_____

_____

_____

_____

_____

_____

_____

_____

_____

_____

2. What have been the biggest changes you have seen in your husband's life over the last year?

_____

_____

_____

_____

_____

_____

_____

_____

_____

3. What are you most proud of about your husband and what are you most excited about?

_____

_____

_____

_____

_____

_____

_____

_____

4. What are the top three things your husband has done "right" or done "well" this past year?.

_____

_____

_____

_____

_____

_____

_____

_____

_____

5. What have been some of your thoughts about the health of your family and your marriage?

_____

_____

_____

_____

_____

_____

_____

_____

_____

6. What are 3 romantic dates you would enjoy in 2007 with your husband? What about the all time "big trip?"

_____

_____

_____

_____

_____

_____

_____

_____

7. What changes are you trying to make about yourself this next year and how can your husband help you?

_____

_____

_____

_____

_____

_____

_____

_____

_____

Friend / Parent Survey

Dear Friend / Parent,

The person that gave you this survey is participating in a personal development retreat. How would you like to play a key role in helping your friend? You can do so by answering the following questions with complete honesty. Upon completion please place your answers in an envelope, and seal it and write his name on the outside and give it back to him. Thank you in advance for your participation.

1. Since you have known your friend / son, how would you say he has changed?

_____

_____

_____

_____

2. If you knew your friend / son was committed to working on becoming a better person, what would be your suggestions of areas that he focus on?

_____

_____

_____

_____

3. What would you say your friend / son greatest strengths are?

_____

_____

_____

_____

4. What are the times when you have seen your friend / son at his best and at his worst?

_____

_____

_____

_____

5. Are there any areas of your life that you want to change that you would like your friend / son to help you with?

_____

_____

_____

_____

6. What are some words of encouragement that you would like to share with your friend / son?

_____

_____

_____

_____

Made in the USA
Monee, IL
01 December 2024

71998023R00132